Praise for *En*

I love this book! Heidi builds ~~~~~ research on emotion and the beauty of Scripture. Her books are know... for being intensely practical and intensely theological, and *Emotions and the Gospel* is exactly that! I am excited to read this book together with my college students. This is a must read for any leader striving to build emotionally healthy disciples.

> —*Megan Barone, director of campus discipleship and outreach,*
> *Holy Cross Lutheran Church, Kearney, Nebraska*

Ever since the angels proclaimed, "Fear not!" Christians have struggled with emotions. Are they good and godly, or are they bad and of the devil? What's a faithful Christian to do: express them or stuff them? In her wonderfully transparent way, Heidi walks with us into the world of emotions: through the Scriptures, her own feelings, and her therapeutic approach. Using a solid biblical basis, she invites us to explore more deeply our thoughts, beliefs, and feelings about emotions. I love this book! You will too!

> —*Rev. James Otte, MDiv, MEd, LPC, associate pastor,*
> *Messiah Lutheran Church, Plano, Texas,*
> *and director of congregation and worker care, Texas District*

This book engaged me from the beginning. I am an emotional person, and I overanalyze most situations. Heidi mingles personal experiences with professional insights to bring understanding and acceptance to emotions. I thank Heidi for recognizing that we are works in progress, designed by God, and covered by His grace. As we struggle with balance, she recognizes that the struggle is real—and okay.

> —*Debbie Larson, president,*
> *Lutheran Women's Missionary League, 2019–23*

God did not create us in His image to be repressed zombies or exuberant phonies. Heidi Goehmann refreshingly validates human emotions as a good gift of God, neither to be repressed nor faked, but to be received gratefully as necessary tools for authentic interactions in a fallen world. In so doing, she not only teaches us about ourselves but also about God, who created us to be like Him.

> —*Rev. Dr. Nathan Jastram, professor of theology,*
> *Concordia University Wisconsin*

Heidi teaches us the importance of searching through Scripture when our cultural experiences come up short. She takes the emotions that we have tried to cram into neat little boxes and helps us give them the space that God intended them to have in our lives. This book helps us reexamine our emotions, not as good or bad, but as helpful, necessary, and purposeful. Heidi gently emphasizes that there is always grace and compassion when we bring our emotions before God, but most important, she helps us build a foundation based on who we are in Christ Jesus, the emotions we experience, and our Creator. The Body of Christ and the overall Church will benefit greatly from Heidi's careful unpacking of emotional research and the importance of emotions rooted in biblical truth.

—*Elizabeth Warren, author, artist, wife, and mom*

In a world of emotional polarization, Heidi Goehmann invites us into a deep and practical exploration of emotions as a gift from God. Drawing on biblical truth, professional understanding, and personal experience, *Emotions and the Gospel* is a timely, holistic, and refreshingly relevant resource for navigating the complexities of life and relationships.

—*Matthew Hein, senior pastor, NewLife Community Lutheran Church,*
Swartz Creek, Michigan

Emotions and the Gospel is a must read for anyone involved in ministry. I can't wait to read it again. Heidi writes like she is having a conversation with you at a local coffee shop, letting you into her own life and experiences, struggles, and joys, all while pointing back to the Gospel every step of the way.

—*William "Shurphyl" Jackson,*
retreats program manager, Camp Luther

The next generation of Christians is crying out for authenticity and connectedness. We can't have either without emotion. Heidi not only explores our God-given emotions but also qualifies them as gifts, even the ones we don't like to talk about in church. The Church gets weird regarding emotions. This book is the antidote. If we desire a deeper relationship with God and a growing ability to connect and love others, that wholeness must include a deep dive into our emotional world. This book is not a substitute for that dive but a toolbox to get the most out of every venture into it.

—*Josh and Sarah McKinley, area directors,*
youth ministry and outreach, Young Life

EMOTIONS & THE GOSPEL

Created for Connection

Heidi Goehmann

CONCORDIA PUBLISHING HOUSE · SAINT LOUIS

Author's Note

This book is not intended to be a substitute for professional medical advice, diagnosis, or treatment. Always seek the advice of a medical or local mental health care provider if you have concerns about your mental health or that of someone you love. This book is intended not for self-help purposes but for spiritual and personal investigation. Research expands what we know about emotions constantly. Your local mental health care providers are trained to meet individual concerns. Your local pastor is a good resource for spiritual concerns regarding your emotional and relational life.

Published by Concordia Publishing House
3558 S. Jefferson Avenue, St. Louis, MO 63118-3968
1-800-325-3040 • cph.org

Copyright © 2022 Heidi Goehmann

Unless otherwise indicated, Scripture quotations are from the ESV® Bible (The Holy Bible, English Standard Version®), copyright © 2001 by Crossway, a publishing ministry of Good News Publishers. Used by permission. All rights reserved.

Scripture quotations marked NIV® are from The Holy Bible, New International Version®, NIV®. Copyright © 1973, 1978, 1984, 2011 by Biblica, Inc.® Used by permission. All rights reserved worldwide.

Scripture quotations marked NASB® are from the New American Standard Bible®, copyright © 1960, 1970, 1977, 1995, 2020 by the Lockman Foundation. Used by permission. All rights reserved. www.lockman.org

Manufactured in the United States of America

1 2 3 4 5 6 7 8 9 10   31 30 29 28 27 26 25 24 23 22

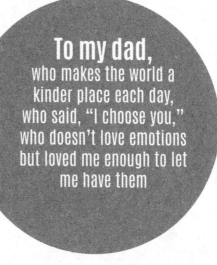

To my dad,
who makes the world a
kinder place each day,
who said, "I choose you,"
who doesn't love emotions
but loved me enough to let
me have them

Contents

Introduction   8

PART 1: Beliefs about Emotions

Foundations of Emotion   18
The Image of God   25
Brokenness and Grace   33

PART 2: Misconceptions about Emotions

Partial Truths   40
Positive and Negative Emotions   45
Too Emotional   49
Unified Facial Response   56
Regulation   61

PART 3: Ways to Process Emotions

About Emotional Processes   68
Contemplation   75
Articulation   84
Exploration   93
Connection   102

PART 4: Specific Emotions

Forgotten Emotions of Scripture   114
Delight   120
Distress   126
Weariness   134
Indignation   141
Contempt   147
Perplexity   155
Felt Compassion   161

Conclusion   169
List of Emotions in Scripture   172
Discussion Questions   175
Acknowledgments   181

INTRODUCTION

Emotions, like many meaningful things in life, are complex. Humanity as a whole seems to have a complicated relationship with them. Do we like them? Which do we like best? Which of them don't we like? Is there a place for all of them? Or none of them?

I notice that we put a massive amount of energy into creating programs and techniques for regulating our emotions, treating them like beasts to hunt and tame. We arm ourselves with tactics rather than compassion or understanding. At the same time, we are intrigued by the concept of emotional intelligence and collecting knowledge related to our emotions. Perhaps, we think, if we learn more about them, we might subdue them or create a "right relationship" with them— though the votes are still out on what that might look like. Our society, like others, has various spoken and unspoken rules about emotion. To some, emotions might be welcome in the therapy room but not in the boardroom. Others believe emotions show up naturally and expectedly in teenagers and women but that men likely have fewer emotions or at least a more natural capability for "controlling" them.

I don't want to condemn any attempt to understand and engage with our emotions. However, I do want to start a conversation about emotions that recognizes their complexity and doesn't try to "solve" them, but instead allows them the space God intended them to have. Theories on emotions abound, but certainty does not. New research on emotions comes out each passing day, and with it, expanding methods for understanding this part of ourselves. The uncertainty of emotions can leave us perplexed, making us uncomfortable and wary of them.

● ● ● ● ●

The Church has a complicated relationship with emotion too. Though many fields of study contribute to the research of emotions, very few theologians study the topic. We leave that to mental health professionals, leadership experts, and occasionally education and character-development gurus. While it's good to rely on capable experts, we miss the full picture when we try to understand emotion only through those lenses. More problematic is that many faith-filled individuals and institutions resist engaging with the concept of emotion, sometimes entirely. There seems to be a belief just below the surface of Western Christianity that favors the false stability of reason and logic, perhaps esteeming them too highly. The undertones of this preference, though unspoken, are clear: Emotion is disconnected from truth. God simply tolerates the emotions of humans. This theological presupposition signals to believers that they should practice Vulcan-esque emotional suppression to please God and to live in righteousness.

Yet, emotions are just as complicated at the other end of the spectrum. In some faith spaces, emotions are celebrated as the foremost evidence of God's presence. Emotions like joy, peace, and gratitude are held up as proof of our faithfulness to God and God's faithfulness to us. But this leaves followers of Jesus with unanswered questions: Where is God when these highly prized emotions are not present in our lives? What happens when struggles like justice and loss bring us face-to-face with anger, restlessness, and anxiety? When pleasant emotions denote God's faithfulness to us, we are left wondering if their absence marks His scarcity.

When pleasant emotions denote God's faithfulness to us, we are left wondering if their absence marks His scarcity.

If God welcomes emotions to be part of our lives, including our spiritual lives, but also doesn't want them to be gauges to determine His presence and constancy, what then do we teach about emotions as a Church?

●　●　●　●　●

In all honesty, I also have a complicated relationship with emotion. All these questions and challenges are my own. I love my emotions and I hate my emotions. Sometimes I find them convenient, warm, useful, and insightful; other times I am challenged by their utter inconvenience, coldness, petulance, and instability. Emotions seem tangible and tamable one minute and completely intangible and untamable the next. I perceive them, I stuff them, I nurture them, I explode with them. They seem to live another life in my subconscious without me entirely.

I have learned and continue to learn each day how to navigate my emotions in healthier ways, but in moments of great emotion, I am reminded of my younger self, a child with big feelings and few skills or words to express them.

When I was six or eight years old, my dad acquired the job of brushing my hair. This was not a moment of beauty or joy or delight for either of us. We had a routine: he would comb and I would cry. Every time, as I felt the tears stinging my eyes, I'd try to hold them back, and every time, those tears managed to spill over and roll down my cheeks.

My dad would ask in the unintentionally brusque voice of fathers who grew up in the mid-twentieth century, "Hey, you cryin'?"

To which my inner response was rage—I wanted to yell at him, "Yes! Can't you see I'm crying? Is this actually a question you want an answer to?" I didn't know that my anger, and likely my dad's too, only masked sadness and shame. That little girl didn't have the language she needed then, and there are moments and days when I don't have the language I need now. We are all works in progress, and so is our relationship with our emotions.

We are all works in progress, and so is our relationship with our emotions.

Perhaps my interest in emotions began on the day my dad changed the narrative of our hair-brushing experience. I don't know what motivated him, but he picked up the brush and moved with intention—he brushed slowly and methodically, bringing love and compassion where before there was unnecessary frustration and shame.

Looking back, I want to tell little Heidi that her sadness and her anger and her angst all have a place. I also want to let her dad know that his sadness and anger and angst can have their place as well. I want both of them to know that love and compassion come *through* these challenging emotions, and kindness and generosity will come from them as well.

● ● ● ● ●

With this book, I'd like to open the conversation about the topic of emotion, not only for deeper understanding, but also to give some attention and space to our younger selves and what we have experienced. While this book is full of information, I also hope to honor each of our individual experiences with emotions along the way.

Emotions are personal. We can always learn more about emotion, but we can only experience the ones inside of us. This individuality means there will be times when your experience with emotions is different from mine. That's good! You'll find more stories for and about my younger self throughout this book as a way to keep us grounded in honoring our experiences with emotion. When you read these, I invite you to ask yourself a few questions:

- What beliefs have you encountered about emotions?
- What are some of your own experiences with emotion?
- When have emotions shown up boldly in your life?
- Are there any places or stories in your life when you wish emotions would have been allowed but instead were uninvited?

This is also a book about the Gospel. It is an invitation to make space and time to understand God's truth, grace, and redemption for our emotions, as written in His Word. Emotions are, at least in part, directly related not only to the character of God but also to the mystery of God, which means there will be a fair amount of mystery to human emotions as well. You will find lots of information in this book about the nature of God and the nature of emotional processes and how they intersect. Neither is simple. We are invited to sit before the Maker and Crafter of all things and ask questions around God's Word and scientific research. With God's hands to guide us and His arms holding us, we are invited to look deeper into God's Law and God's Gospel and look deeper into ourselves to root out the things that need to be rooted out. We are invited to grow.

We will walk through the intersection of emotions and the Gospel with a posture of curiosity, asking these questions together:

- Are emotions valuable to God?
- Are certain emotions desirable or sacred while others are base, to be overcome or cast out?
- What's the "right" amount of emphasis on emotion in our lives? What is too much? What is too little?
- Are there ideal scriptural or scientific methods for working with our emotions? Is there a "right" way to experience emotions?
- How do I help my partner, spouse, friend, or the annoyed customer service agent with their emotions?

As you read, I ask you to consider these questions with a bias toward openness, aware that we won't have all the answers and that the ones we do find together will not be neat and tidy. We will also rely on God's affection for us and His grace to guide us in our searching. The foundational belief of Christianity that Christ died to save us and heal our relationship with God means two things for our relationship with God: God does not expect us to know everything (that's His job), and God knows we need help. He does not judge our need, but rather calls Himself Helper. Take heart in the words of Jesus in John 14:26: "But the Helper, the Holy Spirit, whom the Father will send in My name, He will teach you all things and bring to your remembrance all that I have said to you."

With that in mind, let's reframe the concept of emotions with God's Gospel through Jesus Christ. God doesn't judge our emotions in the way that we do, fingers pointed, inner critic at the ready. Like all of our parts, our emotions are judged by the grace extended to us through what Jesus has done for us. The uncovering and work of discovery in and around our emotions reveals things about ourselves. More than that, with God's Word in our lives and the Helper of the Spirit as our guide, our emotions also reveal to us some things about God, which we'll discover together. God values our emotions, and not only the ones that seem pleasant or "good" to us. They are complex gifts, each with its own purposes. Of course, we can degrade the gifts of God and misuse them. And so, perhaps most important, our emotions often point us to our need and are some of the most powerful reminders in our lives of God's redemption, restoration, and a brighter eternity.

It's a different way of looking at emotions when we stop seeing them as inconveniences or problems to solve. It may seem dangerous to let them have more space even in a discussion, let alone in the practices of our daily lives. Yet, God is faithful, and grace through Jesus Christ is what saves us, not doing emotions "correctly." Jesus' grace through the cross, through the empty tomb, through the Word of God, is what heals us and helps us flourish, change, and grow. There are certainly ways our responses to emotion can lead to unhealth, but God's Law, showing us our imperfection, is meant to be a gateway to God's Gospel. Jesus' love for us in His death and resurrection speaks restoration over every emotion in our lives. With hope and grace and restoration as the endpoint, we can see Jesus' steadfast joy showing up powerfully when we have joy; when we have sadness or anger, we can see Jesus inviting us to sort through it and ask questions and be tended to by Him. His ears are ready to listen to us, His arms are ready to catch us, and His feet are ready to walk with us.

Another layer of Gospel that we don't want to miss here is the gift of other people. God gives us the firm foundation and friendship of Jesus Christ and the counsel of the Holy Spirit and His Word, but He also gives us one another. Research from the field of interpersonal neurobiology tells us that, while suffering does impact our ability to regulate our emotions, sharing our experiences and feeling seen and heard by someone else brings us a sense of integration.[1] We need people in our lives to sort through our emotions with us, but perhaps we might also grow from simply witnessing the hurts and joys of our shared humanity alongside one another.

Note that this is not a self-help book. I am not offering a better or "right" way to experience or express emotions. The purpose of this book is to know more about God and connect more deeply with Him through the lens of our emotions and, in doing so, to learn more about ourselves. This is gentle work. "Fixing" and "solving" ourselves tends to be less gentle work and often creates challenges to seeing God's grace in the midst of our lives.

---

1   Daniel J. Siegel, "The Developing Mind and the Resolution of Trauma: Some Ideas about Information Processing and an Interpersonal Neurobiology of Psychotherapy," in *EMDR as an Integrative Psychotherapy Approach*, ed. Francine Shapiro (Washington, DC: American Psychological Association, 2002), 85–121.

As we work through the topic of emotions together, we'll start with a theological lens to gain some theological foundations, looking at common beliefs and misconceptions about emotions. Then we'll move to a practical or personal lens to gain foundations for processing emotions. Finally, we will use those foundations to walk through some emotions in Scripture that seem to be forgotten, to help us expand the language we use for those feelings when we experience them in daily life.

Throughout this book, there will be information and knowledge and insight. There will be some sorting and some increased awareness. There will likely be conviction because the Gospel and authentic connection in relationship also include accountability and boundaries. Yet, there will be grace because the Gospel in our relationships always includes mercy.

GOSPEL TRUTHS FOR OUR EMOTIONS

- Emotions are complex.
- God is complex.
- It's okay to have a complicated relationship with both.
- The grace of Jesus Christ is available for both our relationship with God and our relationship with our emotions.

PART 1
Beliefs about Emotions

FOUNDATIONS OF EMOTION

My therapist's office in Ohio always smelled like nature in all the best ways. The warm brown leather chairs were cozy, and to this day I think of healing when I see similar chairs.

Therapy is a lot of things, but I would never use the word *easy* to describe any of them. My heart was heavy, my mind filled with thoughts that gave me no reprieve. What stands out most even now about that time was the invisible weight attached to my chest, making it hard to breathe. There is a book called *The Body Keeps the Score*, and I slowly learned the truth of those words in that therapy room at thirty-four years old.

After several visits, my therapist asked me, "Heidi, what if you felt *all* of your feelings?"

I indicated that the world would crumble under my sadness, that the anger deep in my gut seemed to have no room in my home or my church. Instead of feeling, I had asked my body to hold back a tsunami. This vessel, knit lovingly by my Creator, had become a dam keeping at bay all the emotions I didn't think had a place in the Christian walk. I wasn't aware I had built that schema. It was part of a belief system I had picked up along the road of life somehow—even though it did not serve me well, nor did I actually believe it to be true!

I had traded real emotion for forced silver linings, replaced the true and life-giving Gospel with false positivity.

How far had my silver linings gotten me? How distant had God begun to feel because of those weights I had asked my body to hold? These questions opened more: What was the purpose of these emotions that felt closer to brokenness than grace so often for me? What were my values and how did they relate to my emotions? What did I think God wanted of me from feelings?

I needed an emotion foundation.

●   ●   ●   ●   ●

Opening up our emotions can feel like a leap—scary, unknown, a physical and mental commitment. We resist in fear and in buttoned-up put-togetherness that God never asked of us.

This section of the book will ground us in the emotion foundations we need to take the leap. It explores the questions above and is meant to bring us to a place where we can rest in God's truth and grace when we process our emotions, feeling attached to God through them, rather than detached from Him because of them. Our God—Father, Son, and Spirit—is our safety when emotions, perspectives, and experiences shift and the weights we hold in our bodies make themselves known.

●   ●   ●   ●   ●

God is not absent from our bodies. He tends to them and cares for them. Through Baptism, our bodies become the chosen residences of the Holy Spirit. God's creation of our bodies is also His provision. That creation is an intimate process. In Genesis, God formed Adam by putting His hands in the dirt and connecting His mystery to the physical world. Eve was formed with this same connection of God's mystery and the physical material of Adam's rib. These bodies of ours are intricately woven still today by our Maker (Psalm 139:14; Ephesians 2:10). We are made up of complex cells, organs, and tissues; dependent on various fluids, minerals, and micronutrients; and knit with nerves and veins and pathways. There is beauty in the mystery of our Maker meeting the physical thing known as our body with His hands, crafting us miraculously before birth, and continuing to knit what we call our "self" today.

Yet, the "self," this person that is you, is more than a body. God's continuous work of crafting and knitting not only our physical parts but also that broader and deeper sense of self is an important foundation for our understanding of emotions. God made each of us to be far more than a body alone. We have a mind and heart and soul. We have senses and emotions, thoughts and beliefs. These unseen, intangible parts are related to our physical being and together make up who we are. God cares for all of us, soul and spirit and body. God sees us wholly when we have only glimpses below our own surface, and He does not turn His face from any part of us or our experience.

God cares for all of us, soul and spirit and body.

As humans, we experience life in these bodies and with these intangible parts imperfectly. One day, when Jesus comes back to restore all things in His own wild and wonderful way, we will experience what the Bible calls glorified bodies (Philippians 3:20–21). Here God's mystery meets the physical body in a new, miraculous way. Embodiment is to humanity as water is to the ocean. We can maybe picture the ocean without water in it, but would it still be the ocean? We wouldn't be humanity without our unique combination of bodies, thoughts, emotions, and many things seen and unseen, understood, misunderstood, or never quite understood.

Why does this discussion of embodiment matter? Because as humans we occasionally would like to ditch the body for the soul or the soul for the body. Sometimes we elevate our physical selves, giving an abundance of attention to diets and exercise or whatever satisfies our senses in an isolated moment. We're tempted to view health only in the extremely limited sense of what is covered by medical insurance and what supports longevity. At other times, we can elevate our mental capacities, limiting ourselves to our thoughts, wonderings, and judgments. Still other times, we become gnostic and see only the value of our souls and spirits, disdaining our entrapment in these jars of clay, so easily cracked and broken. We also elevate or exclude our emotions. Often we want to push our emotions aside or belittle their role in our life. Other times we give them far more attention than they deserve, making them leaders and determinants of our days.

●　　●　　●　　●　　●

Because emotions are personal, our beliefs about emotion can easily come from only our own vantage point. But emotions exist apart from our experience with them. Emotions originated in God before the beginning of the world, which means that emotions existed between entities before they existed between God and humans or between people. God is a connected community of three persons, or what theologians call the Godhead, mysteriously making only one God. God the Father, God the Son, and God the Spirit exhibit emotions themselves. God the Trinity has pleasure together in the creation of the universe. God the Trinity experiences joy in their fullness of being. God the Trinity was angered and saddened by humanity in Noah's days and I'm sure in our own. And so we encounter another emotion foundation: emotions exist outside of our human experience of them, in the Godhead. Emotions are not limited to what we as humans think, feel, or understand about them.

Emotions are not limited to what we as humans think, feel, or understand about them.

Yet, while emotions exist apart from us, emotions are an essential part of how God made us. Another piece of emotion foundation to lay down is that our emotions impact our interactions with Him and with one another. These emotional interactions have been happening since the beginning of humanity's creation. We are people created by

God with emotions. When God said, "Let Us make man" and He "saw everything that He had made and, behold, it was very good" (Genesis 1:26, 31), that included emotions. In creation, emotions were gifted to us by a good God and were called good as part of that creation. Another emotion foundation we can embrace: emotions are not inconvenient mistakes but rather gifts to be held in our hands.

Sometimes the best way to understand the beauty of a gift is to use negative imagery: to imagine life without that particular thing. For example, author Mari Andrew has compared life without emotions to a blue sky with no sunsets and no place for the twinkling stars to come out and shine.[2] What would life be like without the ability to feel a diversity of emotions in our experiences?

In the beginning, emotions existed perfectly. They served as connectors. Imagine the emotions of joy, awe, humility, and bestowed value and grace moving between God and humanity freely, with no disruption. Before brokenness and its hurts, the human response to God's good gifts, including emotion, was likely thanksgiving and awe in a sense of connectedness. Imagine love and tenderness and understanding moving from human to human without all the heartbreak and tension. Emotion brings into our lives one more way for God to *know* us relationally and us to *know* God relationally. We see this perfection of emotion moving between God the Father and God the Son when the Father says, "This is My *beloved* Son, with whom I am well *pleased*" (Matthew 3:17, emphasis added). We see it when Jesus is full of joy in the Holy Spirit, praising the Father for His plans, His timing, His character (Luke 10:21).

Like the rest of God's good gifts, emotions now exist in the brokenness of the world. Oh, how beautiful it would be if just one part of our lives could go untouched by brokenness! But the entrance of sin into the world means that sin affects everything, including our

---

2   Mari Andrew, *My Inner Sky: On Embracing Day, Night, and All the Times in Between* (New York: Penguin Books, 2021).

emotions. Our emotion foundation here is not only that our emotions are broken but also that we experience them in the brokenness of the world. Disappointment, fear, and sadness exist not because we are sinful but because the world is hard, imperfect, and broken. The good news is that where brokenness is evident, Jesus' redemption is not far away.

Jesus' emotions during His time on the earth in the incarnation, from birth to death, were impacted by brokenness. Yet, He remained perfect. Jesus' experience of anger and sadness, without sin, tells us again that sadness and anger are not in themselves sinful, wrong, or disconnecting. It's easy to make emotion the bad guy here, but at what cost? Saying that emotions can lead us to sin is different than saying certain emotions are sinful. Is it possible that emotions like sadness and anger are still gifts of the Creator? How would we process a broken world without tears? How would we respond to injustice without anger? How would we keep ourselves safe from harm without fear? These things reside with us because of sin's existence in this world, but that doesn't cloak the entire concept of emotion in sin. Nor does it make some emotions sinful because they may only be experienced in the brokenness of the world. Unfortunately, we have a hard time imagining many of these emotions outside of our ability to make a mess of everything. While the relationship between brokenness and emotion is mysterious, God reveals much to us in Jesus Christ.

● ● ● ● ●

As we move on, we'll see more of God's own experiences with emotion in Scripture as He responds to and interacts with humanity. We will learn about God's emotions and build awareness of God in our emotions. Again and again in the Bible, we see God the Father respond with truth and with grace to His Son, to His people, and to humanity as a whole. We see that He is never far off.

Despite how weird and wild they can be, emotions originate within the heart of God. God proclaims all of us—heart, soul, mind, and strength—to be redeemable in Jesus Christ. We have been given these complicated gifts to connect us, top to bottom, soul to body, one to another, a gracious God to the people of His hands.

EMOTION FOUNDATIONS

- God created us as emotional beings.

- Emotions exist outside of humanity.

- Emotions impact our interactions with God and others.

- Emotions are gifts from God.

- Our emotions are broken in this world, and we experience them in brokenness.

- Our emotions, like the rest of us, are redeemed in Jesus Christ.

THE IMAGE OF GOD

Mrs. Harp's fourth-grade class was quiet, each student taking a test of some sort, backs bent over multiple-choice and short-answer questions. My feet could almost touch the floor without trying. Almost.

I remember my pencil stopping above the page as I considered an answer and suddenly having the strongest sensation of my own thoughts within my mind. With the awareness of the hum of my thoughts also came the awareness of the hum of everyone else's thoughts around me. I wondered if their thoughts were different from my own and quickly realized they must be. If we all said our thoughts in unison aloud, would they fill the room with their noise like on *The Electric Company*? Would the sound of our thoughts confuse and overwhelm us? Would our thoughts disappear as fast as they came, like mist, to make room for more thoughts as they came?

I'm guessing these kinds of ponderings are why adults patted me on the head so much as a kid rather than respond.

● ● ● ● ●

We are all thinkers of thoughts. Most people have had an experience like mine, when they became aware of their thoughts as part of their humanity and the commonality of thinking among humankind. As thinkers of thoughts, we each look around us, take in information, and consider benefits and consequences. We often recalibrate based on the information we receive.

Thoughts, however, are not the whole story of our mind and mental processes. Thoughts are connected to other processes in our body. Sometimes we act through involuntary processes: breathing, digesting food, blinking, our heart beating. Other times we act voluntarily: we make a conscious choice to take a certain route, seek out a glass of water when we are thirsty, or open our mouth to speak words with a specific message.

Emotions are part of these involuntary and voluntary processes. They are connected to our thoughts, but they aren't our thoughts. They are connected to our choices but are not our choices. They are their own thing, and they are linked to everything.

Emotions tend to come before our thoughts and actions and then also in response to thoughts and actions. When our heart flutters, we might have a simple sensory experience of it—a butterfly sensation or a short intake of breath. We might have an emotional experience as well—a note of anxiety, maybe a strange feeling of doom, like something is terribly amiss. Take another example: When a loved one cries out in pain, we are quick to jump up and inspect what's happened; our body may react before our mind begins working through possible solutions. We are often flooded with compassion to reach out and help before we consider what kind of help that might be.

Emotions are a necessary part of the processes of our bodies and of life. Our capability to have them and to feel them was knit into us, just like our ability to think, touch, taste, talk, and move. They supply information and connect us to the things we need and the people we love.

●　●　●　●　●

Emotions also connect us to our Creator. They tie us to God in an intimate way: God is an emotional being as we are emotional beings. While we are not the same, we are mysteriously similar in some ways.

Our ability to feel comes not only from God's gifting but also from God's *being*.

Genesis 1:26–27 explains why our emotions are connected to God and simultaneously adds some mystery to the whole process of being human:

> Then God said, "Let us make man in *Our image*, after *Our likeness*. And let them have dominion over the fish of the sea and over the birds of the heavens and over the livestock and over all the earth and over every creeping thing that creeps on the earth." So God created man *in His own image*, in the image of God He created him; male and female He created them. (emphasis added)

God imprints Himself on us. In this way, we are made differently from everything around us. I can remember Dr. Nathan Jastram, one of my favorite Old Testament professors, standing in front of the classroom and teaching us how complicated any discussion of the image of God is. If you are interested in the image of God in general, I suggest his writings, which are grounded in the Gospel and full of biblical insight.[3]

Dr. Jastram taught us to look for Jesus across the pages of Scripture, from Genesis to Revelation. He had a particular affinity for those Scriptures written in Hebrew and taught us to read them through the unique lens of the Hebrew language and culture. Genesis 1:26–27 is a great example of Hebrew superlative, or the tendency of the Hebrew language to repeat important things for emphasis. God's image in and on humankind is important to God. Dr. Jastram also taught us that context matters. The verses around Genesis 1:26–27 emphasize wholeness, or completeness, in the creation account—that creation is

---

3   Nathan Jastram, "Man as Male and Female: Created in the Image of God," *Concordia Theological Quarterly* 68, no. 1 (January 2004), http://www.ctsfw.net/media/pdfs/jastrammanasmale.pdf; Burnell F. Eckardt, "Another Look at *Imago Dei*: Fulfilled in the Incarnate One," *Concordia Theological Quarterly* 79, nos. 1–2 (January/April 2015): 67–78, http://www.ctsfw.net/media/pdfs/EckardtAnotherLookAtImagoDei.pdf.

whole with the addition of humankind to the plants and planets and penguins. There is also a wholeness or thoroughness to God's work of creating, which culminates in His work of creating everything, declaring it good, and then resting.

Wholeness is part of who we are as humans as well. Scripture describes the wholeness of humans with the language of heart, soul, mind, and strength. We were made in God's image, which is a mystery to some extent, but His image isn't limited to our faces or form. He makes each part of us, and His image is an important part of our wholeness. Which parts of that heart, soul, mind, and strength are in many ways parts of Him?

Does your brain hurt yet? The image of God sends my mind whirling every time.

That little girl in Mrs. Harp's class who had lots of thoughts about thoughts also grew up to have lots of thoughts about emotion. If there is an air of mystery and a little heaviness to the image of God and our emotions, that little girl would like to thank you for thinking all the big thoughts along with her.

● ● ● ● ●

It is a beautiful thing to be connected to God in wholeness and also for that wholeness to include our emotions. What is harder and less beautiful is that Genesis 3 crashes in far too soon after Genesis 1 and 2. Wholeness is ruptured. We are scattered people, no longer reflecting God's image perfectly, because the mirror has been broken. This rupture includes our emotions.

God was not ruptured in Genesis 3, and neither are His emotions. Just as God's thoughts are not our thoughts, God's emotions are not our emotions (Isaiah 55:8–9). We experience emotions as fleeting, irregular, and hard to understand so much of the time. God in His perfection, His holiness, His God-ness has a different experience and vantage point of emotions. We experience emotions as indicators of our needs; God has no needs (Acts 17:25). Yet, God experiences desire and longing too (Job 14:14–15; 1 Timothy 2:4).

Just as God's thoughts are not our thoughts, God's emotions are not our emotions.

God and His emotions can be confusing to us because in the rupture there is also now mystery. To understand some of the mystery, we let God's Word show us who God is, including His emotions. Scripture doesn't always discuss emotion in the narrative. But thank goodness it does give us several clear accounts of God and His emotions. We always hold both those pieces together: looking at what Scripture reveals while knowing that Scripture doesn't reveal all. For that revelation, we wait for Christ to return. In Christ, we have what we need now while we continue to learn more each day. This practice keeps us from making assumptions about God and enables us to identify assumptions about God in things we read or hear. When in doubt, go to Scripture and find out more through the truth of God's Word. And know that one day, we'll understand it all completely, including our big thoughts on emotion.

In the Old Testament, we see a wide spectrum of God's emotion, which can feel far off and confusing. In a recent email, Dr. Jastram reminded me that the emotions of God, like our own, are not in a vacuum. God is understood through both Law and Gospel, not one or the other. When we read about God's hate, it helps to know it does not exist outside God's love. When we hear stories that include God's anger, it helps to hold that anger alongside God's delight and patience.

Another thing to remember about emotions in the Old Testament is that they were experienced before the death and resurrection of Jesus Christ. Part of their purpose is to point us to humanity's desperate need for that death and resurrection of Jesus Christ. When you read the list below, how do the emotions of the passage remind you of our great need as humans for Christ's redemption?

- love (Jeremiah 31:3)
- sorrow (Isaiah 53:3)
- anger (Exodus 32:9–10)
- longing (Isaiah 30:18)
- pleasure (Psalm 147:11)

In the New Testament, emotions are often a little more comforting to contemplate. We see a more complete version of God's emotion in God's humanity, in the person and work of Jesus Christ. But even here, Jesus' emotions are not limited and must be viewed through a Law-and-Gospel lens. Where do you see both the Law and Gospel of God in these examples of Jesus' emotional experiences?

- joy (John 15:11)
- troubled (John 11:33; 12:27)
- anguish (Luke 19:41)
- compassion (Matthew 9:36; 15:32)

We see the most complete and perfect image of God through the image of our Savior. As humans who are not God-in-human-flesh as Jesus was, we carry the image of God and the emotions of that image in brokenness. Because of that brokenness, our faces, our forms, our minds, our hearts, and our souls reflect that image inaccurately. Jesus' reflection of God is always accurate.

How might our imperfect emotions give us a window into God's emotional life? There are certainly times we let out the Holy Spirit loud and clear, reflecting God's compassion, warmth, love, and empathy. More often, though, our imperfection acts as a powerful reminder that God is better than anything else we might grasp for or seek. He fills us when we feel depleted. He is what we need when humans disappoint. Human emotions act as a foil to God's constancy and consistency.

The Bible tells us that God doesn't change (Hebrews 13:8). He is steadfast and faithful (Psalm 86:15). He is compassionate, strong, truthful, and just. All of these attributes are worth cultivating in our own character. Often our emotions can feel like a train barreling down the track of our character, making it obvious that God's image is disrupted in us. In the brokenness of the world, God's image, which is holy and pure in Himself, is distorted in us. But the juxtaposition of our imperfect emotional life with God's perfect emotional life isn't about us becoming more holy by having better emotions or better emotional control. Instead, God uses our imperfect emotions to reveal our need for His touch. In Jesus Christ, we have redemption and full relationship with God, and that redemption extends to our emotional lives.

Our emotions glorify God not in their holiness but in their connectedness. They nudge us toward God's presence with humanity. They are reflections of a God who is more than cerebral thoughts and actions. When our emotional experience is connected to God's Word, we see the depth of impact God allows in His relationship with each of us. Emotions may be confusing and dim reflections of an emotional God at times, but that doesn't negate the reflection. Emotions can help us to see God, even if only in part. In the words of the apostle Paul, "For now we see in a mirror dimly, but then face to face. Now I know in part; then I shall know fully, even as I have been fully known" (1 Corinthians 13:12). Emotions are a part of being known, both in the sense of understanding and in the sense of relationship.

●　　●　　●　　●　　●

Knowing in part isn't easy for us, whether in understanding or in relationship. The image of God is a complicated topic. Emotion is a complicated topic. Put them together, and we certainly end up with dissonance, that feeling of discomfort when the pieces of the puzzle before us don't quite fit but we know they do fit somehow. I believe God enjoys our desire to work with the pieces of the mystery, to spend time getting to know Him more and understand Him more each day. God loves that little girl in Mrs. Harp's class, and I think He's enamored with her thoughts about thoughts. He still sits with her in her complicated thoughts about emotions. Eventually, when Jesus comes back, we will know fully. Wholeness will come. Emotional wholeness will come. Until then, our emotions reveal God's ability to bring healing and redemption to what isn't whole and to what doesn't look redeemable. As God promises in His Word, He will make us new in Jesus Christ, perfectly in His image once more:

> I will sprinkle clean water on you, and you shall be clean from all your uncleannesses, and from all your idols I will cleanse you. And I will give you a new heart, and a new spirit I will put within you. And I will remove the heart of stone from your flesh and give you a heart of flesh. (Ezekiel 36:25–26)

BROKENNESS AND GRACE

I planted my first seedling around age 7. My dad was a gardener. As a child, it seemed to me that he envisioned our garden providing food for the whole world, or at least the Western Hemisphere. My dad liked help with his feeding project, but not long after that first plant I lost interest, and Dad found he liked quiet in the garden more than my complaints.

I faithfully avoided gardening until 2017, when we moved into a new home with no landscaping. Where others might plant green things, our home had only rocks and more rocks. I wanted life to grow in my rocks. Our first summer there, I planted cucumbers, peppers, and basil because they sounded yummy and low maintenance—my kind of garden friends.

The bounty exploded, particularly the cucumbers. We became those people who left cucumbers on your front porch without checking to see if you wanted them first. Our kitchen island overflowed with cucumbers.

With expanded confidence in my gardening skills, I planted my trusty bumper crops and a few others the next year. I was undefeatable.

Until I was defeated.

The cucumber plants never produced new leaves, much less vegetables we could eat. That year everything just kind of died. I tended them with care and water and kindness, and they gave me nothing. I obsessed and ruminated until I found myself dramatically complaining to the administrative assistant at our church.

"Oh," she said, "no one's getting anything this year. Sometimes it's just like that with plants."

● ● ● ● ●

And so it is, with vegetable gardening or tending the gardens of our emotional and relational lives. The landscape of this world is wonderful and also broken. The soil feels the brokenness. You feel it. I feel it. It isn't our fault so much as it is our state—sinners in need of mercy, a world in need of forgiveness.

We experience emotions in this brokenness. Just as the land experiences tsunamis and gentle showers, drought and plenty, we experience the weight of what is harsh alongside what is wonderful in this world. When we look closer at ourselves and our perspectives, our complications and our gifts, it's easy to see our emotions are good and also not quite right. They are often misaligned with what we want to communicate, what we long to feel, or who we are.

Another layer of this discussion is the *necessity* of emotions in a broken world. As we experience the pain of brokenness, emotions help us make meaning in it all! God seems to have known we would need joy, laughter, and thanksgiving to offset the turmoil and uncertainty. God brings us delight and warm hearts in our winters and wilderness.

In His grace, God even provides the uncomfortable emotions to help us release some of the heaviness of the world. Fear that wasn't necessary before found a purpose when deception entered the garden and brother turned against brother. Distrust can lead us astray at times, away from God's protective arms, but it also pokes at our conscience when someone is trying to take advantage of us or when we find ourselves in a relationship that does not have God's good in mind. In God's way, He turned what could have been only disorientation and confusion into something for our good. Emotions are not meant to be leaders in our lives. They are not guides or managers. But in brokenness, we need the information they provide to walk forward each day.

●　　●　　●　　●　　●

Our meta-emotions tend to be the most problematic and the most beautiful of our emotions. Meta-emotions are our emotions about our emotions—what we feel about feelings. We enjoy joy; happiness makes us happy. But in a broken world, our meta-emotions also mean that pain causes us more pain, and the anxiety we experience over anxiety is real. What was meant to serve us becomes terribly self-serving. That anxiety about our anxiety and our sadness about sadness cuts at the open wound of life's hardships. As a therapist, I have sat with so many humans to help them hold together their great disappointment in humankind's universal inability to escape the unfaithfulness of our emotions and sometimes the actions we let them guide us toward.

That anxiety about our anxiety and our sadness about sadness cuts at the open wound of life's hardships.

When challenging emotions and the life circumstances that bring those emotions press in, we can find ourselves wondering why God feels so far away. If emotions are meant to help us express all that needs to be expressed in a broken world, why do they leave us feeling separated from Him? If emotions were given to make our lives more manageable, to give meaning and comfort in their own way, why do they sometimes seem to lead us not to God's comfort but to His sorrow?

Take the story of Jonah in the Bible. People tend to talk about him like he needed a second chance, but the truth is he needed a fourth and a seventieth chance, just like us. It's striking to me that the root of Jonah's issues wasn't necessarily his emotions of fear or anger or bitterness, though he had these in spades. (Solidarity, man.) At the end of the day, Jonah was disappointed in disappointment, and he was disappointed in who God was. He grumbled at God's very character and God's expression of that character through His mighty and mysterious emotions. In Jonah 4:2, Jonah gets incredibly honest with God:

> And [Jonah] prayed to the LORD and said, "O LORD, is not this what I said when I was yet in my country? That is why I made haste to flee to Tarshish; for I knew that You are a gracious God and merciful, slow to anger and abounding in steadfast love, and relenting from disaster."

I can almost see Jonah under his shade tree, shaking his fists at the sky, pointing his finger at the God of the universe, raging about the undeniable existence of God's mercy and love. Disappointment in disappointment will do that to a guy. Meta-emotions can be friendly companions or our own worst enemies in brokenness.

● ● ● ● ●

There is yet another layer: the brokenness of emotions between people. God is mercy and *feels* mercy toward people we think undeserving. We all have our Ninevites. Brokenness rears its head. Being created in God's image gave us beautiful access to feeling all the lovely things. It also gave us access to feeling all the lovely things toward one another. But brokenness eats at our experiences and our relationships. It can leave us exhausted and dehydrated in the hot sun of life, much like Jonah was. We can find ourselves annoyed that God's experience of emotions is so perfectly beautiful, so full of mercy, so slow in anger, so consistent in love. While God experiences His emotions perfectly, we can become tired of how complicated we are—and the complications of all the people around us.

In the weariness of our emotional landscape, God gives us a tree, some shade, maybe a bench. He invites us to stop and consider our internal experiences. He doesn't ask us to stuff them down, throw them out, or negate them. When confronted with our deep and difficult emotions (and even the more pleasant ones), God provides a space that says, "You are Mine. Take your time. No need to respond quickly. Sit with it. Wrestle with it. We'll figure it out together."

God is process oriented. We tend to be unrealistic about who we should be and what we should think and do. We want to have the perfect image of God in every essence—thoughts, emotions, minds, souls, to the depth of our core and the tips of our toes. Instead, God offers space and the safety of His arms to hold our complex and broken selves. He doesn't need us to understand it all today, to have the perfect emotional expression today and each day. He redeems all of us, toes, core, heart, mind, and soul. God's perfect Son came to take all our pain, all our shame, all our sin, and all the rest of the story, including our emotions. He experienced all the emotions. He understands all the emotions.

Through Baptism, Jesus brings His clear and wondrous redemption into our lives. God also designed amazing processes in our bodies to bring that redemption into our lives in striking ways. He gives us tangible gifts as reminders that He hasn't left us alone in this space, simple yet complex things such as water poured over our heads in His name, bread and wine holding body and blood, the faces of other believers, the vulnerability of those willing to wrestle with truth in love. God gives us His Word for stability, so that in our questioning and confusion we know where to find Him. Through His Word, we can distinguish God from the world, truth from confusion, grace from the voice of our inner critic. God crafted these things to give us not just a space for emotions, but a *safe* space. They are the shade trees of our desert experience.

Emotional processes and emotional maturity will take all of us some time, but our gentle God is mightier than time. Time, too, is touched by His grace. Even if it doesn't come today, there's still room for growth.

PART 2
Misconceptions about Emotions

PARTIAL TRUTHS

I believed in Santa Claus until I was thirteen. My parents and I would leave out chicken nuggets for the Big Guy in Red every Christmas Eve. I am not sure how this tradition started, although I'm guessing it had something to do with missing cookies one year and an open drive-through on the way home from church. The single nugget with one bite out of it left on the plate meant exclusively for Santa cookies was pretty convincing. Even more convincing was the gnawed reindeer carrot leftover in the morning.

The truth is I only half believed in Santa Claus my whole life, and my parents knew it. The unique comfort of a half-truth is likely why we kept up this charade for so long. We could talk about visiting Santa at the mall and how unbelievable his beard was and talk about what he and Mrs. Claus did after the holidays all in one conversation. We could collect the treasures requested on the Angel Tree at the back of the church, knowing that Santa isn't the answer to the world's problems, and also mail letters to the North Pole at the special green postal box downtown.

● ● ● ● ●

The dispensation of reality is so very comforting. As humans, our reality is a broken world, and that brokenness creeps into everything. We cling to ideas like Santa Claus or zero-calorie meals because they make that reality a little easier to bear. Our psyches can only handle so much struggle, even with the joy of Jesus in our hearts, so we paint murals on the concrete walls of our lives—choosing one-dimensional cover-ups—when it's too hard to look at the real deal.

This system of almost reality or mostly reality obviously has its drawbacks. We try to comfort ourselves with half-truths in the more serious areas of life. At times we forget or choose to ignore full reality when we really need to acknowledge it. It takes work to challenge ourselves, to dig deeper and ask questions. The myth is pleasant in some way, shape, or form and serves us well when we want to escape the complicated. Offering fun half-truths might be fine with Santa Claus or fairy gardens, but the half-truths we allow or perpetuate about emotions are less beneficial.

Santa began as a real person. St. Nicholas hailed from Lycia (modern-day Turkey). He was a bishop of some sort in the Christian Church and was extremely generous and principled.[4] As it is today, poverty was real and shocking during St. Nicholas's place and time. When we consider the fact that not all children will have presents for Christmas, coupled with all the other junk of the world, we turn to our trusty defenses and design comforting stories like Santa or Narnia or Marvel movies. This can be a good and helpful way for us to process life's challenges. Other times, when these stories become what we believe and apply to others, it serves us better to hold half-truths up to the light—to enjoy them for what they are but speak reality back into them as well.

● ● ● ● ●

Consider how a half-truth is made: When humans encounter a complication, we try to make sense of it by breaking it down. This usually starts off well with theories and insights that lead to discussion. But often something gets left unsaid or left out. Instead of recognizing a complicated truth with all its facets, we turn a part into

---

4   Julie Stiegemeyer, *Saint Nicholas: The Real Story of the Christmas Legend* (St. Louis, MO: Concordia Publishing House, 2007).

the whole, making "truth" out of something that could *possibly* be, something that *might* be, something that *may* be true. We oversimplify the facets because we prefer a solid answer, a solution, a place to put our focus. We share our half-truth with a friend, or a friend shares it with us. Public speakers start sharing the half-truth. The half-truth makes its way into graduation speeches and books. We start teaching it to humans who are smaller and younger than us. Families pass the half-truth down. At times the half-truth sort of works, and so it continues without a whole lot of question. The half-truth feels cozy and comfortable.

When humans encounter a complication, we try to make sense of it by breaking it down.

At the end of the day, a half-truth still means that one half is false. Even with nuggets of truth, even when half-truths help us make sense of something, even when they make us feel better, they are not reality. It is actually better for our mental and emotional health when we find ourselves dissatisfied with half-truths. When we accept half-truths as whole, our subconscious usually knows better. Our inner workings try to get our attention, usually in the form of anxiety or exhaustion. It's as if they're hollering, "Red flag! Something is off. Pay closer attention! Primary systems need attention."

For example, think of the exhaustion that comes when we make "Choose joy!" our refrain. "Choose joy" can be good, but often this emotional expectation cloaks two half-truths: (1) We each have a choice in everything. (2) The only correct choice is joy. But what of the value or purpose of sadness, guilt, or frustration? Joy is good. Joy is also not all we were made for. Our bodies and minds know that there must be a place for more. Often without meaning to, we neglect to honor our sadness or struggle—or someone else's—by "trading up" for joy. The full truth that we can embrace in Jesus is that struggle and joy can coexist, and He is not absent from either of them. Baptized believers have the enlightening support of the Holy Spirit, but we were all knit with a conscience and an emotional compass. We were designed to cry when we are sad and laugh or smile when something delights us. We can dull our emotional compass just as we can dull our moral conscience, but it will still try to get our attention. *all are different*

Which emotional half-truths are most prevalent today? Which perpetuate most easily? Usually we end up with the ones most convenient for the current culture, those that make sense for what we're facing at the time. The Greeks perpetuated misconceptions related to Stoicism because they revered the thinkers of the day who encouraged Stoicism, and a country of flagrancy could use a little Stoic reasoning. More recently, misconceptions created by the concept of manifest destiny show us that some partial truths are more dangerous than others. What might have started as good intentions for spreading the Gospel turned into something convenient for building power in Western empires. I use this as an example because it helps us see the danger of partial truths, especially when they're wrapped in good intentions. A tiny seed can grow into something huge and far-reaching, whether a mustard seed of faith or falsehood. In our present day, we perpetuate misconceptions around our mental health, such as "Just get outside!" or "Eat well and that will solve it *all*!" We want simple answers for topics that are anything but simple.

We also easily forget that we learn new things about our emotions every day. Research uncovers things we didn't know before, and it can be difficult to integrate those discoveries when they contradict what we thought we knew. When new information exposes a popular half-truth about emotion, especially one we have believed for a long time, our collective consciousness rises up with the shame of being "wrong" or "uninformed" or "having missed something." These thoughts and emotions are so burdensome that we ignore the truth rather than

different cultures try to dictate emotions

learn something new. We perpetuate the half-truth more strongly to cover the shame.

●　●　●　●　●

If this all sounds dramatic, it is because these emotion misconceptions have victims—particularly children asked to put their emotions away, women left to believe their voices have no place, and men asked to bury nurturing and connection for confidence and bravado. Half-truths about emotion may serve us, but they don't serve us well.

When we hold on to culturally perpetuated half-truths and expectations, we miss out. We miss out on the gift of new insights through the truth of God's revelation. We give up the meat of relational wrestling in favor of the chicken-noodle comfort of hiding our shame. We forgo the forgiveness and grace that comes with confessing we are only human and always learning.

In the next chapters, we will finish laying a foundation for emotions by examining some misconceptions about emotions. We'll confess our humanness and our struggle to find truth in this wonderful but broken world. As we uncover half-truths around emotion, we stand in the redemption of Christ and look toward learning, growth, and His healing. There is no shame in His redemption, only revelation.

I felt like a platypus pastor's wife

POSITIVE AND NEGATIVE EMOTIONS

Humans love to classify things—genus, species, Latin names, Venn diagrams, diagnostic labels, archetypes. You name it, we can come up with a system and neat little boxes for it. I do like understanding things more clearly. I like organization. However, we can take our demand for systems past their usefulness. Take the platypus for instance—it has a bill and lays eggs like a bird but produces milk like a mammal.[5] It doesn't fit our categories, no matter how hard we try. Our emotions are a bit like the platypus. We can classify them all we want, but they aren't neat and tidy.

● ● ● ● ●

In twenty-first-century Western culture, our favorite classification system for emotions is positive and negative. Some psychologists and mental health professionals tackle the conundrums that this oversimplified system presents, but as a whole we love "good" emotions and hate "bad" emotions.[6] Which emotions would you consider positive—ones you enjoy, that help you live a thriving and happy life, that feel comforting? Which emotions would make your negative list—ones that exert negative influence on our mental systems, that tax us and leave us empty, that might cause us to fall into some kind of temptation?

If I used this sort of system, here's how my list might look:

---

5   "Platypus (*Ornithorhynchus anatinus*) Fact Sheet: Taxonomy and History," San Diego Zoo Wildlife Alliance Library, last modified August 10, 2021, https://ielc.libguides.com/sdzg/factsheets/platypus/taxonomy.

6   See, for example, Todd B. Kashdan, "The First Myth about Positive Emotions," *Psychology Today*, March 3, 2015, https://www.psychologytoday.com/us/blog/curious/201503/the-first-myth-about-positive-emotions.

POSITIVE	NEGATIVE
happy	sad
joyful	angry
laughing	hurt
excited	opinionated
relaxed	jealous
content	irritated
calm	shameful

Is your list different from mine? Comparing lists in black and white can be useful to see where a system built on the idea of positive and negative emotions breaks down. Did someone's happiness lead to your sadness? Did contentment keep you from pursuing something you were called to do for a time?

What of the beauty when we empathize with someone's sadness or when a friend shares our sadness alongside us? When anger alerts me to injustice, is it negative or positive? Emotions are anything but simple. This partial truth becomes more dangerous for Christians when we equate emotions our culture considers negative with sin. I have sat with many Christians as they wrestled with a long-held subconscious (or sometimes conscious) belief that their sadness or distrust was offensive to God. They want to know if their irritation or jealousy separates them from God. Our emotions certainly impact our relationship with God, yet you'd be hard pressed to find lists of emotions God proclaims as negative or positive in the Bible. While some emotions are more likely to cause problems for us (I'm looking at you, anger),[7] there is something very Ecclesiastes about a time for anger and sorrow, a time for laughter and rejoicing.

do ugly emotions separate us from

---

7 Jeffrey Gibbs, "The Myth of 'Righteous Anger': What the Bible Says about Human Anger," Concordia Theology.org, October 19, 2015, https://concordiatheology.org/2015/10/the-myth-of-righteous-anger-what -the-bible-says-about-human-anger/.

God?

who created negative emotion, were they like golden

Marc Brackett, research psychologist and author of *Permission to Feel*, uses the language of positive and negative emotions. However, he points out that it's useful to feel and navigate those negative emotions, particularly stress. Pervasive or intense stress can cause our brains to overactivate, which is particularly problematic if it occurs when we're young. Brackett states, "What research now shows is that different emotions serve different purposes for learning. . . . Negative emotions have a constructive function: they help narrow and focus our attention. It's sadness, not happiness, that can help us work through a difficult problem."[8] Other researchers give time and energy to the work of uncovering the cognitive and affective components of emotions—that is, the interaction between our thoughts, beliefs, and emotions. This more rounded approach shows how categories like positive and negative aren't so easily distinguished for single emotions.[9] Each emotion we experience as humans has positive and negative reverberations. They refuse to be neatly boxed.

I've learned from mentors as well as from my experience as a therapist that perhaps a better way to reflect on the classification of emotions is as an individual. Labeling our emotions for what they are *for us* can be an insightful experience—not so we create our own subjective truth about emotions and twist them every which way we'd like, but so we can understand our own natural response and judgment toward emotions as they come up in our system. A paradigm shift I have heard in the psychological community is to consider whether certain emotions are challenging or comforting to us, rather than positive or negative. It can be surprising which emotions feel uncomfortable, confusing, and scary to some people and which feel pleasant, enjoyable, or safe.

---

8   Marc Brackett, *Permission to Feel* (New York: Celadon Books, 2019), 29.
9   See, for example, Sieun An et al., "Two Sides of Emotion: Exploring Positivity and Negativity in Six Basic Emotions across Cultures," *Frontiers in Psychology* 8 (2017), https://doi.org/10.3389/fpsyg.2017.00610.

When we remove judgment from our emotions, we generally find them more manageable.[10] We can hold them gently, step back from them, and look at them from enough distance to let them inform us.[11] This distance keeps them from holding the power of leadership. Most of us have a list in our back pocket of emotions that feel "good" or "bad"; we also might have a list of emotions we think God believes are good or bad. Is the picture we paint one of God standing over us demanding better emotional balance? Does that image align with the redemptive heart of God in the person and work of Jesus Christ? We don't want to oversimplify God, but we do want to keep the redemptive and restorative nature of God at the forefront of any conversation about Him. In our emotions—any emotion—we are invited to pray with the psalmist, "Turn to me and be gracious to me, as is Your way with those who love Your name. Keep steady my steps according to Your promise, and let no iniquity get dominion over me" (Psalm 119:132–133).

Even when our emotions are challenging, God's posture toward us is grace in Jesus Christ. The Gospel motivates us, never the Law within ourselves. As emotions present themselves in our lives, whether internally or in the face across from us, may that grace reign. God, in Christ, is with us in our emotions, whether they challenge or comfort. Each emotion has its purposes, and God can do His work through whatever comes at us or in us. He is God of the good, the bad, the positive, the negative, the comforting, and the challenging, gracious to those who love His name.

---

10 Lane Pederson, *Certified Dialectical Behavior Therapy Professional Training*, PESI, accessed August 12, 2021, https://catalog.pesi.com/viewer/classroom/4953278.

11 Susan David, *Emotional Agility* (New York: Penguin, 2016).

TOO EMOTIONAL

At age 25, I was the mother of two small children. Three things seemed certain each day when I woke up: my deep love for my sweet little family, ever-intrusive daydreams of grad school, and doubts and fears about my new role as a pastor's wife. These were beautiful and turbulent days soaked in the gentle affection of fuzzy baby heads but also filled with postpartum anxiety and depression. My emotions felt like a fire-breathing dragon living just beneath my skin.

As happens in life together in a community of faith, I happened upon a disagreement with someone. The topic is irrelevant; what matters is that, for the first time, I heard the phrase "too emotional" spoken aloud and directed at me. Someone said something brusque and blunt, in the strange assumed intimacy that often occurs in congregational life. Tears rimmed my eyes, and I didn't know how to respond. With my baby on my hip, I walked away just as the tears started coming full force. I pushed my way to the bathroom, but not quickly enough. The last words I heard before stepping into the safety of the ladies' room: "She's far *too emotional.*"

●　●　●　●　●

Years later I came to understand this as another half-truth: the idea that emotions are unwelcome and out of place in public and sometimes even in private. "Too emotional" also rears its head through an unspoken idea that there is a threshold of acceptance for emotions. Who determines what is and is not acceptable with emotions in public or private? At what level are emotions acceptable? The misconception of "too emotional" implies that some are in the know and are right about emotions and their place, while others are outside the norm.

We often see this partial truth through passive-aggressive looks, side comments, or exclusion. But who determines what emotional balance looks like? Both Scripture and scientific research support a wide array of emotional expression, whether in private or in the place of close community. When we refer to someone's boldness as anger, we end up with the idea of "too emotional," as if anger is ruling the person, when he or she often has made a calculated decision to express thoughts and feelings together. When someone begins to tear up and we avert our eyes, we engage in the half-truth of "too emotional." How often do we communicate "too emotional" because we're uncomfortable with a *certain* emotion? How often does it happen that we're uncomfortable with *any* emotion?

Who determines what emotional balance looks like?

In Western culture, the phrase "too emotional" is usually directed at women. Through some lenses, intentional and unintentional, women are seen as having more emotion than men. Other lenses suggest that women are prone to inconvenient expression of their emotion or that women lack the ability to control their emotions. Research does show some differences in how men and women experience emotions. Women consistently report stronger expression of their emotions, while men report stronger internal experiences with certain emotions.[12] The research is still out on which emotional differences between men and women are biological and which are learned culturally. As Christians, we fall far too easily into assumptions about male and female. Part of interpreting the Bible means exploring which aspects of being male or female are set in us by God and which are

---

12 Yaling Deng et al., "Gender Differences in Emotional Response: Inconsistency between Experience and Expressivity," *PLOS ONE* 11, no. 6 (2016), https://doi.org/10.1371/journal.pone.0158666.

Andrew works very hard to always be

simply cultural expectations. For the cultural expectations, we must ask ourselves as individuals, how healthy are those expectations? As psychology does its work in figuring out emotional health, may we also do our work as God's people to further understand how God made us.

●   ●   ●   ●   ●

The Bible gives us a wide lens of the human experience, which can be useful to help us find firmer grounding about the emotional differences between men and women. God's Word shows men and women displaying a variety of emotions. Consider Hannah's prayers for a child in the temple, so heartfelt that her tears flowed and the priest, Eli, thought she was drunk (1 Samuel 1:10–17). Eli's assumption seems to be that Hannah's deep emotions are out of place in God's house, or that because her emotions are uncomfortable they are therefore inappropriate. Yet, Hannah's prayer is so moving that you can find it in baby nurseries across the United States. The story of Hannah praying reveals the influence of a particular cultural lens through which we view emotion.

Peter is a man of great emotion in Scripture. He consistently jumps forward with confidence or rashness, depending on the situation. Luke 22 in particular shows the breadth of Peter's strong emotional responses. Also consider Paul's description of his and his companion's experiences in 2 Corinthians 1:8: "We were so utterly burdened beyond our strength that we despaired of life itself." Paul, Peter, Hannah—all heroes of the faith and all vibrant people of emotion.

The phrase "too emotional" is also commonly used as a microaggression or microinvalidation aimed at minority groups. Microaggressions or microinvalidations are subtle—or sometimes not-so-subtle—jabs endured by minority groups based on the broader population's cultural assumptions and biases. Microaggressions may be used to judge others who are different from us in any way, including people whose emotional experiences are different from our own. Examples of people most likely to use microaggressions in the Bible include Haman in the Book of Esther and the Pharisees in the four Gospels. Haman targeted the Jews living in Babylon and targeted Mordecai directly. The Pharisees targeted Jewish sects or believers they saw as "lesser than." Both Haman and the Pharisees eventually took matters into their own hands, using direct oppression of some kind, seeking the lives of those who threatened their ideals or stations, but first came the smaller blows and assumptions. A quick read through the Gospels reveals places where the Pharisees' half-truths led to destruction.

God's people can examine themselves around cultural half-truths and bias with the Gospel of grace as their companion. God's Word and His Holy Spirit are always available to us and never forsake us in hard conversations. With these two things among us and the mercy and grace of Christ within us, we can address cultural half-truths that find their way into the Church.

God's Word and His Holy Spirit are always available to us and never forsake us in hard conversations.

I was at a church meeting once when the topic of discussion was whether women should serve in church leadership. For those who said no, their primary reason didn't have to do with the Bible or doctrine but rather because women are "too emotional." These were people I loved and who deeply respected and admired me and other women in their midst. Yet, the microaggression of "too emotional" was alive and well, intentionally or unintentionally. This is the danger of perpetuated misconceptions and why I call them "partial truths." Do people, including Christians, get caught up in our emotions and let them lead us? Certainly. Do we sometimes let emotions rule our lives and lead us to relational destruction? Absolutely. But do emotions still have

are emotions (especially negative)
something that need to ~~JOO EMOTIONAL~~
out?

their place in our communication, whether in our families, at work, in our communities, or in our church meetings? Yes, they do.

● ● ● ● ●

Emotions are present in all of us all the time. How many meetings have you sat in where you can feel the emotions in the room but no one speaks them aloud? It's tempting to believe our thoughts and actions are guided by logic and reason only, those pieces of ourselves that are more comfortable in our culture.

Yet, reason, logic, and emotions are not the distinct entities we'd like them to be.

A history lesson might help us see how "too emotional" became a powerful partial truth. At various times throughout history, our human discomfort with emotion caused us to seek the supposed stability of reason. The Greek Stoics and then the Enlightenment thinkers of the eighteenth century sought to sever emotion from reason using daily practices and thought exercises. This planted the idea that emotions need to be held at bay in order to have an educated conversation. With the Industrial Revolution, we also began to prize progress and productivity. Emotions became inconvenient and uninvited guests at the progress party. Who can move forward when someone is fiery with anger? Quotas and production lines are disrupted by family strife or grief.

While emotions might limit us at times, our discomfort or silence around them can also be limiting. For example, we can express a fiery, intense belief without throwing reason out the window. In fact, higher emotional intelligence correlates with more productivity at work and higher earnings.[13] Perhaps the emotion of compassion might help us

---

13 Melody Wilding, "3 Myths about Emotions at Work You Need to Stop Believing," *Forbes*, August 17, 2020, https://www.forbes.com/sites/melodywilding/2020/08/17/3-myths-about-emotions-at-work-you-need-to -stop-believing/?sh=547771f851ac.

better express ourselves both at home and in the workplace. Empathy is well documented for its many benefits in homes and organizations.[14]

It is challenging to live in a culture where we are constantly concerned that if we display a tiny bit of emotion, we might be viewed as "too emotional" or without reason. We can let our emotion meet our reason, let them overlap and touch, and do the work of helping us be whole people taking informed action, valuing the full human experience, and connecting all of it to a good God of both truth and grace.

● ● ● ● ●

In dialectical behavior therapy (DBT), there is a concept called wise mind. Wise mind has two necessary parts: emotion mind and reason mind. The reason mind represents our logic and practicality; it is oriented toward facts and rules. The emotion mind is oriented toward our moods, urges, pains, and pleasures. We are more likely to act wisely when we engage both emotion mind and reason mind. In this model, emotion and reason are held in tension, necessary companions working together. They overlap. They have their areas of expertise but aren't completely distinct. They work together to create a full mind, a *whole* mind. Interestingly, when Jesus references our heart, soul, mind, and strength, such as in Mark 12:30, the Greek term for "mind" encompasses not only reason but also broader ideas of insight and balance. The biblical concept of the mind involves movement, reaching through or between or across.[15]

We can bring this partial truth into a fuller truth by honoring the emotion in the room, allowing it to be there, while also allowing reason its space. Saying or implying nonverbally that someone is "too emotional" is incredibly invalidating. Validation is an essential build-

---

14 Jill Suttie, "Why the World Needs an Empathy Revolution," *Greater Good Magazine*, February 1, 2019, https://greatergood.berkeley.edu/article/%E2%80%8Bitem/why_the_world_needs_an_empathy_revolution.

15 Strong's Concordance, s.v. "1223. dia," https://biblehub.com/greek/1223.htm; Strong's Concordance, s.v. "3539. noeó," https://biblehub.com/greek/3539.htm; Strong's Concordance, s.v. "1271. dianoia," https:// biblehub.com/greek/1271.htm.

ing block to conversation and connection. To validate is to recognize the plausibility or accuracy of someone's distinctly personal experience. We might have a different personal experience. We might have a hard time seeing what someone has experienced or is experiencing. We might completely disagree with the person's perception of their experience. Validation stops to recognize that difference and respect it. We can validate even when we don't agree. We can validate even when we have very different experiences.

Saying or implying nonverbally that someone is "too emotional" is incredibly invalidating.

Validation is especially important when we communicate about someone's emotions. It is true that someone is sad or frustrated or ecstatic, even when we ourselves don't feel those things. And people are allowed to feel how they feel. We are unlikely to change that for or with them. Experiencing the depth of someone's emotion with them is a powerful part of relationship, and one we especially want to have within the intimacy of the Body of Christ. Recognizing the emotions in the room, both our own and other people's, brings the grace of validation to the moment. When we give emotion its space, reason and practicality can often meet us as well. Invalidation pushes those things away, leaving us without the needed tension between emotion and reason.

Over time, I have learned to allow my tears to come both in private and sometimes in public. There is no shame in a good bathroom cry, but in our culture we sometimes need to fight to give emotions a little more space when they rise to the surface. Even though our emotions show up uninvited at times, we can bring more connection and better communication when we pay attention to them along with reason. There is full truth in this: we were made to be emotional.

UNIFIED FACIAL RESPONSE

In those early days of being a mom to tiny humans and getting my feet wet as a pastor's wife, in between diapers and dreaming of grad school, I began volunteering as a peer counselor at our local pregnancy center. I taught one-on-one courses with expectant moms, dads, or couples about pregnancy, birth, and child development. I learned a lot myself in every session.

One video lesson showed all the different involuntary responses babies have—such as how babies will turn their head sideways, extend one arm, and bend the other at the elbow in a "fencer pose." I had no idea that babies experience several of these universal involuntary actions as they grow. Another video explained that babies mimic the facial expressions of their caregivers, showing a mom sticking out her tongue again and again and the baby trying relentlessly to mirror her action. It also showed babies watching a parent make one expression or another and the baby being disinterested or making a different expression, which the parent then mimicked. My clients and I learned the importance of the relationship between a young child and caregivers and that natural growth comes from that intentional connection.

● ● ● ● ●

The theory of unified facial response states that humans have a set group of facial muscles that help us express emotions nonverbally. The scientific conclusion, then, is that because of this universal human expression of emotion, certain "basic" emotions are easily translated between humans. For instance, you smile, so you must be happy. You furrow your brow, so you must be angry. Many researchers follow this idea to some degree. Yet, other researchers argue that it's not so simple. The more we discover in the field of neurobiology and with functional magnetic resonance imaging (fMRI), we find that maybe facial muscle responses are a little different from person to person, and maybe especially different from culture to culture. Lisa Feldman Barrett, in her book *How Emotions Are Made*, introduced the theory of constructed emotion. This theory purports that while we are wired for sensory input and react to that input in the form of emotion, the *way* we react to, experience, and understand it is not entirely predetermined. Barrett's team conducted research with remote tribes of a non-Western culture, and their work revealed that those people attributed facial expressions to emotions quite differently than people in Western cultures do. We sometimes need to widen our view and look at other cultures to see the biases of our own.[16]

Humans are more complex than we like them to be.

The bias toward universal facial expression might actually show our cultural bias toward the work of Charles Darwin. Barrett traces the concept of unified facial response back to Darwin's research and work published in *The Expression of the Emotions in Man and Animals* in 1872, where Darwin exposited that there are specific categories of emotions distinguishable by facial expression.[17] This work was originally intended to connect emotional expressions to survival and the evolutionary process. Like Darwin's other research, while not without its contribution, this research on expression is biased toward his evolutionary model and is not meant to provide a comprehensive foundation for the way emotions are experienced and translated

16 Lisa Feldman Barrett, *How Emotions Are Made: The Secret Life of the Brain* (New York: Mariner Books, 2018).

17 See Paul Ekman, "Darwin's Contributions to Our Understanding of Emotional Expressions," *Philosophical Transactions of the Royal Society B* 364 (December 12, 2009): 3449–51, https://doi.org/10.1098/rstb .2009.0189.

across humankind. Humans are more complex than we like them to be. It may be comforting to overapply research and data to understand our complexity, but a better starting place for good science is with a posture of curiosity, further inquiry, and an awareness of our limitations. This is also a more honest posture before our Creator. God's words in Job 38:4–7 remind us of our limitations, even as God reveals more to us all the time:

> Where were you when I laid the foundation of the earth? Tell Me, if you have understanding. Who determined its measurements—surely you know! Or who stretched the line upon it? On what were its bases sunk, or who laid its cornerstone, when the morning stars sang together and all the sons of God shouted for joy?

I include unified facial response as a partial truth about emotion because it shows our desire as humans to control and simplify what we cannot understand. Not everything is true, which means we need to be honest about what we know is true and what only might be true. As humans, we want our relationships to make sense, we want to know how best to communicate with other people, we want some solid ground to stand on in a changing world. The half-truth of unified facial response is comforting because it means we are a little more same than different, more easily understood when so often we find ourselves misunderstanding. While we do have lots of commonalities as humans, it is good to question whether we can understand one another at literal face value.

Emotions are both voluntary and involuntary. While we share emotions through our facial expressions, we can use expressions to hide them as well. Our genetics are part of the story—there is some universality to the human experience. But culture and social conditioning also affect how we understand and express our emotions. Both are true. Complex truth is better, even when we don't fully understand it, than oversimplified half-truths.

●   ●   ●   ●   ●

Scripture gives us freedom in our emotional expression. In the poems, narratives, and even lists within God's Word, we see people processing the physical load of emotion in a variety of ways. The Bible often expresses emotion through a wide range of physical descriptions:

- faces aflame (Isaiah 13:8)
- bones wasting (Psalm 32:3)
- waist/stomach constricting (Isaiah 21:3)
- hot heart (Psalm 39:3)
- head bowed (John 19:30)
- gnashing teeth (Lamentations 2:16)
- sick at heart (Jeremiah 8:18)

Many of the emotional expressions in the Bible are also culturally indicative of the main people groups in the Bible. While we don't want to turn the Bible into a scientific study of the facial expressions of humankind or minimize it into an anthropological study, it is living and active in many ways that lead to truth. It broadens our view, giving us a wider lens than only our own culture. Again and again, God shows us through His Word the complexities of humankind rather than the simplicity of humankind.

●   ●   ●   ●   ●

The field of affective neurobiology has opened many new windows to understanding our brains, bodies, emotions, and the connections between all of them. While sitting beside clients at our pregnancy center, I had no idea that one day we would be talking about concepts like mirror neurons. The American Psychological Association describes mirror neurons as "a type of brain cell that respond equally when we perform an action and when we witness someone else perform the same action."[18] I remember reflecting to a client how wildly complex God made us and the tiny humans who are entrusted to our care.

If we believe we were knit together by God's hands, might that knitting happen in different ways? Is it far-fetched to believe that some of the knitting happens when we are formed in the womb, while other knitting happens as we are formed in our specific cultures and families? Could some of our emotional responses be "unified" among humankind while others are more nuanced from culture to culture, family to family, and person to person?

Instead of assuming a completely unified emotional process and response, we can turn to our friends or loved ones and ask what they are feeling and seek to understand their experience. It takes work and energy to ask, to reflect, to reply, and to continue reaching into one another's lives, but we receive a depth of emotional and relational wealth in return. Let's be awed by God through what we know and through what science reveals. Let's be honest about what is theory and what is truth and seek to know one another better through both.

---

18   Lea Winerman, "The Mind's Mirror," *Monitor on Psychology* 36, no. 9 (October 2005): 8, https://www.apa .org/monitor/oct05/mirror, used with permission. See also Sourya Acharya and Samarth Shukla, "Mirror Neurons: Enigma of the Metaphysical Modular Brain," *Journal of Natural Science, Biology and Medicine* 3, no. 2 (2012): 118, https://doi.org/10.4103/0976-9668.101878.

REGULATION

I have kids, so I've spent a fair amount of time on playgrounds. One playground visit sticks out in my memory. We've all experienced a moment when we don't just need to go to the bathroom, we need to go *now*, especially as children when our systems are still maturing. One of my kids alerted me that it was bathroom time. As we headed in that direction, suddenly the world stopped and my four-year-old was on his knees and belly, hands over his ears, rocking back and forth in earnest.

The moment was so shockingly dramatic that compassion took over when there might have normally been annoyance.

I bent down and spoke close to my child's face. "Hey, buddy, what's up?"

"That swing makes me feel loud inside."

Ah, the squeaky swing. I could hear it now, rusty metal against metal, begging for some oil. I thought, how often does something make me feel loud inside too? How often is my inner world impacted by the noise and drama of the outer world? More important, how often do I fail to notice?

● ● ● ● ●

Emotions are often uncomfortable because of the *iceberg* of emotion. When tears come, when fear makes the hair stand up on our neck, or when the wash of pleasure comes with receiving a present, we might be able to identify the emotion we're experiencing in the moment. Sometimes emotions live right on the surface, hard to hide, begging for our attention, like the squeaky swing. Yet much of our emotional life lies below the surface: the prick of annoyance that wasn't worth getting into, the flash of disappointment we move past so quickly it almost wasn't real, the didn't-notice-because-we're-so-busy loneliness, the weariness that lack of sleep brings, the worry and judgments circulating around our brains any given minute. These mostly go unnoticed and unrecognized. They might lie outside our consciousness or on the foggy edges.

Our bodies regulate all these emotions, whether above or below the surface. Based on past experiences, genetics, and intensity, our bodies decide to some degree what does and does not get our attention. Emotional regulation is not unlike nutritional regulation, where our bodies decide what we need, what stays, and what goes, based on what we have needed before and what is happening in the moment. We can all give a shout-out to our bodies and to the Creator of these amazing bodies for being so magnificent.

There are things our bodies need to learn as we grow from childhood and throughout adulthood, one of which is how to move through our emotions. Social emotional education is an ever-expanding field of special interest to parents and school systems everywhere. How do we help children (and adults) learn to regulate their emotions, to regulate themselves?

In its broadest sense, emotion regulation is a good pursuit and necessary to live in the world, to know ourselves, and to have healthy relationships that don't revolve around us 100 percent of the time. But at times, we take emotional regulation too far. Consider nutritional regulation again. We can regulate our nutrition to such an extent that we end up depriving our bodies of the calories and nutrients we need. We become weak, frail, unwell. The same is true with emotional regulation. When "control" and "manage" is the only language of emotions, we tend to *overregulate* them in unhealthy ways instead of gently training our body toward emotional wellness.

● ● ● ● ●

If you look up definitions and details about current emotion regulation strategies, you'll likely find the word *modulate*. Modulating our emotions is about exerting influence over them, adjusting their amplification or the "loudness" we feel inside, and maybe giving them a different tone with new information.[19] Modulating is not the same as controlling something, whipping it into shape, forcing it to obey our commands. Our attempts at controlling our emotions usually only lead to more emotional turmoil or an overload of meta-emotions.

> ## Our attempts at controlling our emotions usually only lead to more emotional turmoil or an overload of meta-emotions.

We have all experienced moments of emotional dysregulation, feeling so overwhelmed by our emotions that we briefly lose our capacity to respond, interact, learn, and grow. The experience or consequences of emotional dysregulation can be unpleasant enough that we want to put our emotions, and the emotions of our loved ones or co-workers, under lock and key.

Often we are best served by investigating emotions rather than regulating them. This language of investigating is common in the therapeutic community but less so in the average home, workplace, or school. Introducing and using this language in daily life will help us dispel the ineffective and potentially shame-inducing beliefs we may have about emotional regulation. My friend Dr. Kim Marxhausen, an educational psychologist and researcher, reminds me that investigating is an important part of regulating. In most social-emotional

---

19 *APA Dictionary of Psychology*, s.v. "Emotion Regulation," accessed December 15, 2021, https://dictionary .apa.org/emotion-regulation.

learning, kids are taught to look for and name their emotions before they "do" anything with them. The "doing" work of regulating can be important, but when we overemphasize the "doing" of regulation we can end up overregulating.

Overregulating is the often unintended consequence of a culture that lacks compassion for the growth of children and the growth of people in general. When we don't encourage investigation of emotions and overemphasize doing something with our emotions, we send the message of "get it together" or "your emotions are not welcome here," which translates to "*you* are not welcome here," whether we mean to or not. Children learn to stuff their emotions down and then grow into adults whose brains have perfected the art. How many children and adults are taught that sharing emotions is part of being in a genuine relationship, with God and with one another? Do we allow the people closest to us to be a bit messy with their emotions? If we don't allow people to feel in spaces that teach and share about God, how challenging might it be for them to believe that God's love is not dependent on how we feel?

Our experience regulating or modulating emotions is not only internal. Co-regulation is another important aspect of growing in our emotional lives. Co-regulation has to do with the way we respond to one another, both verbally and nonverbally, and with involuntary physical processes. Co-regulation is me connecting with the person in front of me struggling through a bad day or me working to understand the person I disagree with instead of ignoring or disconnecting from the emotions they are exhibiting that make me uncomfortable. The concept of co-regulation is especially supported in polyvagal theory, which states that our ability to regulate or exert influence over our emotional state (that is, to use emotions as informants rather than leaders) is heavily influenced by whether the environment is safe for our emotions.[20] Do we get support in our emotions? Do people help us have them and/or understand them? Are we afraid and wondering what will happen if we display an emotion?

The biblical account of Hagar is an emotional one. Hagar was Sarah's handmaiden, but she and her son were sent away from all they knew because Sarah, you might say, was uncomfortable with her own emotions. Genesis 21:8–21 details Hagar's dismissal. What I'd like to note here is God's response to Hagar as she hides her son and weeps over their fate, which appears to be growing worse by the minute. God honors both Hagar and Ishmael with a promise, but first He allows her to have her emotions. He is not uncomfortable with them but asks questions and brings Hagar to the knowledge of her safety in His presence:

> Then she went and sat down opposite [her son] a good way off, about the distance of a bowshot, for she said, "Let me not look on the death of the child." And as she sat opposite him, she lifted up her voice and wept. And God heard the voice of the boy, and the angel of God called to Hagar from heaven and said to her, "What troubles you, Hagar? Fear not, for God has heard the voice of the boy where he is." (Genesis 21:16–17)

● ● ● ● ●

Regulating surely has its place. There is good work to be done inside these minds, bodies, and spirits. As followers of Jesus Christ, the Holy Spirit is never far from us. With the Holy Spirit living in us,

20 Stephen W. Porges and C. Sue Carter, "Polyvagal Theory and the Social Engagement System," in *Complementary and Integrative Treatments in Psychiatric Practice*, ed. Patricia L. Gerbarg, Philip R. Muskin, and Richard P. Brown (Arlington, VA: American Psychiatric Association, 2018), 221–40.

we have a co-investigator, a co-regulator, with us each day in every emotion.

But what do we do when we are dysregulated and don't know where to go to find comfort? What do we do when the swing is so loud we can feel it inside our bodies, or when our pen-clicking, loud-talking co-worker wants to have twelve meetings that could have been emails? What about when we are overwhelmed, angry, or full of sorrow, regret, or bitterness? God is here too. The Spirit is not far off.

We want people to be with us in our moments of deep emotion and dysregulation, and we want to help those we love in their moments of trouble. We want to build safe spaces where God's love and kindness are louder than our own discomfort with emotions.

In the next segment, we'll spend time identifying four basic responses that may be helpful for regulating and moving with our emotions. We'll look at places in the biblical narrative where we see these responses in action, and we'll also look at some research for why these might work so well for our bodies. With these emotion foundations in place, we can work together to build those safe spaces for emotional depth and become more comfortable with the emotions deep inside of us.

PART 3
Ways to Process Emotions

ABOUT EMOTIONAL PROCESSES

When I became a therapist, I never expected to learn so much from my clients, especially the kids in my practice. When I ask a kiddo what a certain emotion looks or feels like to them, they often act it out or use descriptions I would never have dreamed up. I have seen sadness depicted as rain, trains, and ghosts. I have seen happiness as rainbows, fire, and grass. I've heard anxiety described or drawn as "ants in my chest," "bouncing balls all over the place," and, from one teen, "a million people screaming for my attention at one time."

A regular therapy conversation might go like this:

"What does anger look and feel like to you?"

"Hmm . . ." A moment of contemplation from the child.

"What if we draw it?" I might suggest.

Insert sketching and shenanigans.

"It's a blue dinosaur, Heidi."

"Ooh, tell me more. Why is anger like a blue dinosaur? Where does the dinosaur live in our bodies when we're angry?"

"Angry is so big it fills up a whole room, a whole HOUSE, Heidi! And angry is sad too. People don't want to be angry, but they can't help it. It's there taking up the WHOLE HOUSE. It jumps out of your chest, JUMPS OUT!"

Anger does take up the whole house at times, doesn't it? Sometimes it simmers inside of us and other times it feels more like an explosion. And it usually has an emotional companion hiding beneath its weight—sadness, a sense of injustice, maybe love.

Children have their own extraordinary wisdom.

● ● ● ● ●

As adults, we are often frustrated that concrete names and fully understanding our emotions seems just out of reach for our brain. Kids are not as easily influenced by rigid ideas of how things *should* be described and are therefore better at describing things *as they see them*. Much of psychologist Carl Jung's research focused on outlining the way humans use archetype and metaphor to process their world. Jung found that it serves humans in many ways to process our stories, our lives, and the world around us by examining them from a distance. Archetypes and metaphors allow us to produce this distance, which gives us the comfort or even confidence to look more closely at our struggles.[21] Many play-based methods of therapy are built on this theory that humans are made for metaphor and metaphor can help us heal.

I want to invite you to process your emotions with both a realistic lens and a bit of distance. The compassion and grace Jesus Christ offers us through His death and resurrection redeems our emotions gone awry and also gives the freedom to process in a variety of ways, rather than one "right" way.

It's time to build our emotional processing toolbox together.

You already have some tools in your toolbox. Maybe you like to process your emotions verbally, with a friend over a cup of coffee. Or maybe you know that your best time to think through things is in the morning. Maybe a hot shower or a jog helps you come down from an intense discussion. Maybe you keep a journal or drive home from work blaring Eminem or Brahms, depending on the day.

Our emotional processing toolbox is not a system. These are not suggestions for what is right and wrong in your emotional life, nor what is righteous or holy. Rather, the toolbox we build will offer some options that we see in Scripture. Research also affirms these tools.

---

21 E. A. Bennet, *What Jung Really Said* (London: Schocken, 1966).

These emotion-processing concepts allow us to give space to our emotions while building awareness of how our emotions can help us or fool us. The end goal is always connection: connecting to God's truth and grace by honoring what is inside of us, confessing what we need to confess, and celebrating growth.

These are just a few options to put into the toolboxes we're building. There are always more tools to acquire, and some tools may not serve you well personally. Let's start by listing the tools you already have in your toolbox. Make a list of things that have helped you with your emotions in the past and things that you know haven't been helpful. Your list will look different from mine. Emotions are universal, but we experience them individually. A blue dinosaur might accurately reflect your anger, but it also might be a tiger, a smoldering wick, or whatever you imagine that I cannot.

● ● ● ● ●

After we build our toolboxes, you can use whatever tool works for you at a given time. All four of the tools I offer in this section are ways people consistently process their emotions before God in the Bible. Simply because something is in Scripture doesn't make it healthy for us though. Scripture tends to describe the human experience rather than prescribe how we should live our lives. As we explore what the people and passages of Scripture reveal about emotional processing, some ways to apply that knowledge will serve us well; other ways don't feed life and health.

We each also have biases, and it's important to acknowledge those, particularly when we study and discuss Scripture. As I researched and found the four methods of processing I offer in this section, I was influenced by these particular psychological theories and therapeutic methods: the Jungian theory mentioned earlier; play-based methods of therapy; the adaptive information processing model associated with EMDR therapy;[22] narrative therapy and research on the importance of telling our stories; and a lens of self-compassion, validation, and interpersonal communication associated with dialectical behavior therapy and Gottman relationship methods. Of course, theories and research can be skewed. One of the reasons I tend toward these lenses, however, is because of their focus on the incredible capacity of humans to heal. I believe God made us for resilience and growth, but also for healing and restoration.

I believe God made us for resilience and growth, but also for healing and restoration.

Let us set our feet firmly on Scripture and find connection with God around our emotions. Let's also be curious about how the world and our bodies work. Holding these two pieces together—connecting to God through Scripture and curiosity around our own emotional processing—is a good place to start a journey toward strengthening our health and well-being.

Throughout Scripture, we see these four tools for emotional processing:

- Processing through **contemplation**: taking time to notice our emotions and the sensations inside of us and occasionally giving further thought to them
- Processing through **articulation**: using words to express, name, and describe our feelings, sensations, and emotions, as well as allowing ourselves to feel our emotions fully and ask questions about them to understand them better
- Processing through **exploration**: using movement to recognize and release the tension, weight, or exuberance of the emotions, sensations, and feelings within our bodies

---

22 EMDR stands for eye movement desensitization and reprocessing. It is a psychotherapy method designed around accessing memory networks to process the experiences of our lives and their associated sensations, emotions, thoughts, and beliefs.

- Processing through **connection**: intentionally offering our emotions to God and sharing them with others, rather than disconnecting or withdrawing from others and ourselves in our emotional experience

The blue dinosaur example from the beginning of this chapter uses each of those tools for emotional processing. Our kiddo is invited to notice and consider the emotion rising to the surface. They are also invited to articulate it in words or whatever expressive medium works for them. All of this is done between two people, holding the emotion of the moment together. This time of connection around emotion creates better understanding for one or more of the individuals, but also growth in the relationship. In our lives, our emotional processing may not look like a therapy room most of the time. We may not draw our emotions or have a therapist to prompt us to further expression. But we can bring contemplation, articulation, exploration, and connection into our moments for fuller emotional processing in everyday life.

In the coming chapters, we'll take an in-depth look at each of these processing tools, find examples for putting them into action, and consider how they might fit into our already full lives.

● ● ● ● ●

It's tempting to avoid emotional processing because it feels vulnerable. Avoiding our emotions may seem like the safer bet. We protect ourselves with something called defense mechanisms. Life in a broken world does require some protection, but may we cling to the tether of God's grace when we are tempted to protect ourselves in our own ways with our own ideas. The Bible is riddled with faithful people trying to respond to life and its problems with their own ways and their own ideas. It is oddly comforting to see heroes of the faith who both glorify God and use defense mechanisms at the same time. There is grace for when we avoid, defend, and rely on our own strength to bring health instead of relying on honest reflection and God's mercy. Jesus' salvation is for more than heaven. It's for today. We can look our emotions in the eye because God doesn't look away from us, no matter the emotion or experience.

May we cling to the tether of God's grace when we are tempted to protect ourselves in our own ways with our own ideas.

The Book of Psalms is a great example of how humans combine emotional processing and defense mechanisms. The psalms are full of honest reflection, telling the truth of our human condition alongside God's grace and redemption, whether in battle and victory or in everyday life. They also include incredible detail about the person's situation, feelings, and defenses, which reassures us that we're not alone in our struggles. Consider the emotional life of King David, who wrote many of the psalms.

David ruled the nation and people of Israel long before Jesus came to walk with us in human form. David had everything he wanted and yet something was missing. He may have felt lonely, despondent, disappointed, desirous, or bored. We learn in 2 Samuel 11 that he had an affair. David worked extremely hard to live in denial of that affair and likely repressed a lot too—two common defense mechanisms. In the very next chapter of Scripture, God sent Nathan to David—connecting him to someone honest, trustworthy, and compassionate. By sending Nathan, God connected David back to Himself through confession. In Psalm 32 and Psalm 51, we hear the honest outpouring of David's heart and emotions before God over this part of his life—crushed bones, judgment, deceitfulness, desire, a cry for wholeness, restored joy, and more.

The emotional processing in this book offers a similar space. Let us drop our defenses before God and learn how we might grow beyond simply coping. Let's allow for some blue dinosaur moments and, in the process, see God at work in us. Let's see God bringing life, redemption, and freedom into our whole lives, including our emotions.

DEFENSE MECHANISMS

These common defense mechanisms keep us from processing our emotions:

- Denial—keeping reality out of our awareness so we don't have to look at it.

- Repression—unwittingly keeping things in the unconscious to protect ourselves from reality's impact.

- Projection—claiming our emotional experience is someone else's, often because it is unacceptable to us in some way.

- Regression—returning to a younger stage of development to counteract the stress of a current situation.

- Displacement—finding a way to satisfy an impulse with something other than the actual emotional target.

- Sublimation—replacing what we consider to be unacceptable emotions, thoughts, and actions with what is socially acceptable.

 Disassociation—switching our focus to something other than what is requiring emotional energy at the time.

- Humor—if everything is funny, then it can't harm or hurt us.

CONTEMPLATION

Some of my most treasured memories are of fishing with my grandpa. Grandpa had some serious fishing methods that included rolling white bread into balls for bait and occasionally digging in the fridge for hot dogs when they just weren't biting. I suspect Grandpa took me fishing more to teach me the art of contemplation than to catch a big one. Fishing with Grandpa meant quiet and togetherness. It was about the beauty and interest that nature offers. Grandpa taught me something important without really saying it: sometimes if we talk too much, we get in the way of connection and growth.

● ● ● ● ●

Contemplation doesn't sound too intimidating at the outset— more like bookish and peaceful. But as I was taught by my grandfather between two fishing poles, I can easily get in the way of contemplation. I can be noisy and busy and uninterested in frivolous things like being and connecting. And when I do seek the peace of contemplation because the world is busy and hard, I expect to get something out of it. I want to understand through my contemplation. I want to learn things. While understanding can come through contemplation, understanding and learning are not the goals of contemplation.

Contemplation has its biblical roots in Psalm 46:10: "Be still, and know." Contemplation is the act of sitting still long enough to be impacted by or aware of connection, particularly our connection to God. Contemplation is the act of thinking deeply but also reflectively. In contemplation, we sit with something a little longer than we would normally. Contemplation forces us past the surface of a thing, looking closer at the inside and the underside. In contemplation, we look at a thing to *know* it better, not necessarily to know more *about* it.

There is a reason that be still and know of the Psalm 46 variety is so challenging. Both being still and being known are intimately connected with God and His mystery, as well as our own—things our defense mechanisms are attuned to and work hard for us to avoid. Contemplation itself is emotional.

We cannot contemplate without first noticing something or allowing something into our consciousness that we'd prefer to keep in our unconscious. Many things in life are uncomfortable to look at honestly. So it is with emotion. Psalm 46 is a battle psalm, a reflection of the broken things of life, the harshness of the world, and all the emotions that go with those things. Before Psalm 46 ever gets to the "be still, and know" part, it starts with honest grief over the changes and tumultuous nature of life:

> God is our refuge and strength, a very present help in trouble. Therefore we will not fear though the earth gives way, though the mountains be moved into the heart of the sea, though its waters roar and foam, though the mountains tremble at its swelling. (vv. 1–3)

The psalm honestly addresses fear, trembling, rage, and desolation along with gladness and courage in the next verses before the conclusion: "'Be still, and know that I am God. I will be exalted among the nations, I will be exalted in the earth!' The LORD of hosts is with us; the God of Jacob is our fortress" (vv. 10–11).

● ● ● ● ●

When we notice something and then sit with it longer, we begin to notice more. We see nuances and details, colors and facets we would never have seen without the light shining on it. You might try this exercise: Set the timer on your phone or other available device for one minute. If you are feeling brave, try two minutes. Sit quietly and still. Notice what is going on inside of you—thoughts, digestion, sensations, emotions, and the like. Pick up whatever details you can of those internal workings. There is much more going on inside than we are aware of in all our movement and busyness.

Researchers Max Bazerman and Daniel Kahneman both note the hurry of our time and how it impacts our ability to notice what's going on inside of us, leading to challenges with thinking and decision making.[23] Might this struggle to notice, this lack of stillness, in our current culture also impact our ability to notice our emotions?

Contemplation is the act of stretching the time we have available for God and for the things that matter to us. Contemplation is a pause. It might involve conversation, but it definitely involves quietness from the bustle of our day. We often look for what God is doing around us. Contemplation notices God's work in us internally through the Holy Spirit and how our emotions and thoughts interact with the Spirit's voice. Contemplation is an act of stillness, noticing God and our connection to Him. Unlike other emotional processes, contemplation is about internal work that may become external. Contemplation focuses on the noticing and thinking before they ever become words or action.

Contemplation is a theme throughout Scripture. People contemplate in various ways, thinking and praying. They ponder, they watch, they ask questions, they are rebuked and rebuke others, they mourn, and they commit themselves to God and His hope. Not every

23 Max H. Bazerman, *The Power of Noticing: What the Best Leaders See* (New York: Simon & Schuster, 2015); Daniel Kahneman, *Thinking, Fast and Slow* (New York: Farrar, Straus and Giroux, 2013).

instance of pondering in Scripture is about emotion, but sometimes it is. We're not always privy to the emotions in the background of a biblical account. Below is a short list of passages where we see people being curious about their emotions through contemplation or see Jesus inviting us to be curious about our emotions.

- ponder (Psalm 4; Luke 2:14–20)
- watch (Psalm 141; Matthew 26:37–39)
- ask (Psalm 119:81–88; Luke 11:5–13)
- rebuke (Psalm 6; Matthew 16:12–14)
- mourn (Psalm 35; Matthew 5:4)
- commit (Psalm 10:12–18; Luke 23:44–46)

As we practice noticing what's going on inside of us, one important tool to build is our emotion vocabulary. We'll first build our vocabulary about what emotions are, then around naming specific emotions, and finally around the physical experience and intensity of those emotions.

We tend to use the words *feelings, emotions,* and *moods* interchangeably (including in this book). Feelings, emotions, and moods do have lots of overlap, but they also have some distinct features.

Feelings are where our vague emotional experience and our physical sensations meet, and they gradually or suddenly make us aware of what is going on inside of us.[24]

Emotions are where our physical sensations and emotional experience meet our thoughts and beliefs. When feelings connect to our thoughts, we can evaluate and consider them further. Emotions are short term and may be intense.

Moods are created when emotions linger, and they're often less intense. Our emotions become a state of mind not necessarily

24 "The Difference between Feelings and Emotions," WFU Online Counseling, accessed July 13, 2020, https://counseling.online.wfu.edu/blog/difference-feelings-emotions/.

directed at a certain stimulus.[25] For instance, the emotion of grouchiness may come after a bad moment or bad day, but when it continues, it becomes a mood not necessarily linked to that bad moment.

The word *affect* (or *affects*) encompasses all these words—feelings, moods, emotions, and the like.

My grandpa didn't teach me specific terms like affect, mood, and emotion. I learned when he invited me to practice contemplation with him. However, when emotions feel larger than they are, it does help to apply specific language. Giving language to something takes what seems vague and nebulous and makes it more manageable. We experience a sense of agency or control when we can work with our emotions instead of feeling like they control us.

● ● ● ● ●

We can build our emotion vocabulary further by recognizing our individual emotions—which is a challenge, because we rarely experience a single emotion by itself. When we feel anger, we likely also hold sadness, annoyance, hurry, frustration, longing, happiness, or some other emotions underneath. As we learned with our emotion foundations, God made us to be complex beings. Our emotions, like the rest of our selves, will never be as simple or clear cut as we wish, but it's worth taking time to sort through them by contemplating them.

Research tells us that our body reacts differently when we notice our emotions. Emotions that we notice don't activate our body's response systems in the same way unrecognized emotions do.[26] This appears especially true when we name them, which we will talk about in the chapter on articulation.

---

25 Saam Trivedi, "Emotions, Moods, and Feelings," in *Imagination, Music, and the Emotions: A Philosophical Study* (Albany, NY: State University of New York Press, 2017), 9–30.

26 Brackett, *Permission to Feel*, 109–10.

Our body reacts differently when we notice our emotions.

One of the purposes of emotion is to give us a way to react to our experiences. Consider this metaphor: We are all emotional pots set out on the stove of life. In a world that is broken and challenging, the heat is turned on. With more experiences and interactions, the heat cranks up. The flames of stress and pressure can bring up the temperature on the stove quickly. Using contemplation to process our emotions, noticing them and eventually naming them, can lower the heat and keep the pot from boiling over. God's Word, the love of those closest to us, and experiencing compassion and kindness also help to keep the pot at a lower emotional temperature.

When we aren't able or don't have the time and energy to recognize the emotions bubbling inside of us, our emotional intensity rises. The pot starts to boil. Even great experiences, the highs of life, might make emotion bubbles in the water. Left unrecognized, one emotion bubbles up and another and another until they cannot be ignored. We call this emotional layering. Sometimes the pot boils over on the stove. Without tending, our emotions will get our attention one way or another.

Contemplation doesn't need to take hours out of our life. It can be quick and even messy.

"Ah! I want to cry right now. What am I feeling inside of me? What is going on around me?"

"I received a card in the mail just because. I feel warm all over. It reminds me that I'm loved and valued."

"That person is riding my bumper. Oh yes, I can feel that bit of fire in my belly. It makes me angry when people don't follow a reasonable flow of traffic."

"I nailed that project at work. I feel taller today. I'm proud of my work. I'm thankful for the gifts God has given me."

Remember that we grow in this skill as we use it, but we won't be perfect. Often we fail to bring compassion to our experiences. Contemplation might bring our inner critic to light. If you feel overwhelmed with shame or frustration with yourself when you start noticing and contemplating your emotions more, I recommend reading Psalm 18 and Psalm 22 together. This normalizes the scattered experience of our emotions. The psalmists here unabashedly glorify God with their fears and questions alongside their firmness of faith. The presence of both in the Word of God reminds us that God does not need us to have our emotional lives "put together" to come before Him in contemplation.

Sometimes we notice our emotions for a second, give them a quick thought, and then move on. A quick contemplative thought and moving on may be all we have the energy or time for in that moment. But that quick thought is equivalent to seeing the tip of an iceberg. When we have the capacity to notice an emotion more fully and take time to contemplate, our bodies will thank us. We are turning the heat down on the pot by recognizing more details and nuances of our emotions.

● ● ● ● ●

Contemplation can be intimidating in the way that being still always can be. When I was fishing with my grandpa, thoughts tended to pour in; some I liked a lot and others, not so much. We won't always like our thoughts or feelings. They often reveal more to us than we might like. And sin will be wherever human beings are. In this way, contemplation can serve as a form of nonverbal confession, opening our hearts to God for examining. Sometimes He'll reveal what is beautiful and good. Sometimes He'll reveal the gunk of sin. Often He'll reveal both. When Jesus equates the emotional experiences of lust to adultery and hate to murder (Matthew 5:21–30), He invites us to process the presence of these challenging emotions in our lives, rather than ignore them and let them lead us down a path we don't want to take. As with confession, contemplating our emotions, especially the challenging ones, brings us before God in honesty to receive His grace.

In Christ there is no condemnation (Romans 8:1). His compassion offers us much-needed safety around the concept of emotions.

Christ also empathizes. He has been there. He walked as a human, noticed His own hurt, frustration, delight, anger, sorrow, and more. Hebrews 4:14–16 changes the way we interact with even our most complicated emotions, because it clarifies how God interacts with all of our emotions:

> Since then we have a great high priest who has passed through the heavens, Jesus, the Son of God, let us hold fast our confession. For we do not have a high priest who is unable to sympathize with our weaknesses, but one who in every respect has been tempted as we are, yet without sin. Let us then with confidence draw near to the throne of grace, that we may receive mercy and find grace to help in time of need.

God notices our emotions. He walks alongside us in each of them, never leaving or forsaking us. The death and resurrection of Jesus Christ brings reconciliation not only in our spiritual lives but also in our relational lives, our mental lives, and our emotional lives. Jesus creates a safety net for us so we can be curious, feel our feelings, and begin to give them language. In contemplation, we rest in His arms, safe and secure, no matter our emotional temperature. In His arms, we find stillness, we find connection, and we find growth.

CONTEMPLATION 101

Emotional contemplation is noticing and being curious about our emotions in the safety of God's grace. Through contemplation, we can

- build our emotion vocabulary;
- recognize the sensations of emotion;
- connect the sensations to our thoughts, opinions, and beliefs.

Consider these questions:

- Am I experiencing a particular feeling, emotion, or mood right now?
- What three emotions presented themselves most often in my life in the past week?
- What do I *think* about the emotion I am feeling in my body right now?
- What grace does God offer for this emotion?

ARTICULATION

My library card has been a trusty companion since age 9. When I visited our local library as a child, the librarians provided me with their (mostly) rapt attention, undaunted by my tenacious chatter. I remember one day sharing the joy I had found in live professional theater. My parents had recently taken me to see my first show: *Evita*, based on the life of Argentina's famous former first lady Eva Perón. After listening patiently to all my many details, the librarian asked me a question that made my world burst open: "Have you ever read one of her biographies?"

Biographies, the magical world of other people's worlds. The librarian walked me to a section of the library I had not traversed before, where the shelves were so tall there were step stools for reaching the thick volumes at the top. In addition to giving me the gift of a new, magical world, the librarian also taught me two important life lessons:

- Children are capable, far more capable than we usually imagine them to be.
- People's stories matter, and it is a powerful thing for both the teller and the hearer when someone's story is told.

● ● ● ● ●

Children are miraculous. They are new to this world; their internal systems are fresh. Because of this newness, some sensory and neurological systems are more sensitive, more responsive, in many ways than in those of us who are fully grown. This sensitivity can make them hyperaware of noisy lawn mowers and vacuum cleaners at nap time, dissatisfied with a freshly wet diaper (can you really blame them?), or easily moved to tears, tantrums, giggles, or joy. While a tantrum on the grocery store floor doesn't necessarily look like a strength, there is a gift in feeling our feelings fully, especially when the tantrum is met with the grace-filled, boundary-defining response of a trusted adult. Over time, and with more gracious contact from those trusted adults, we learn how to express and articulate our emotions without lying down on the cold tile of the local produce section. (Mostly.)

Kids often do the work of articulating their emotions without noticing them first! Adults model and teach them how to connect the dots, and we teach them better when we ourselves are connecting the dots. Processing our emotions through articulation means giving words and signals to express our emotions, moving them from the inside to the outside. Articulating our emotions means digging deeper to ask questions about each emotion and getting to know our particular version of it. Giving words to emotions also helps us tell our stories and hear the stories of others, trusting that God is working throughout the narrative, in the emotional highs and lows.

Research tells us one of the most useful things we can do to process our emotions is to name them.[27] According to the research of Brené Brown, we regularly experience at least thirty core emotions, but most of us can name only three of them as we are experiencing them.[28] Rather than *worried* or *overwhelmed*, we might simply say *anxious*. Rather than *frustrated* or *irritated*, we might say only *angry*. We also might say nothing at all about what we are feeling.

---

27 Jared B. Torre and Matthew D. Lieberman, "Putting Feelings into Words: Affect Labeling as Implicit Emotion Regulation," *Emotion Review* 10, no. 2 (2018): 116–24, https://doi.org/10.1177/1754073917742706; Carrie MacMillan, "Why 'Social and Emotional Learning' Is So Important for Kids Right Now," *Yale Medicine*, November 6, 2020, https://www.yalemedicine.org/news/social-emotional-child-development.

28 *The Dare to Lead Glossary*, s.v. "Emotional literacy," accessed March 11, 2022, https://daretolead.brenebrown.com/wp-content/uploads/2018/10/Glossary-of-Key-Language-Skills-and-Tools-from-DTL.pdf; Belinda Luscombe, "Brené Brown Thinks You Should Talk about These 87 Emotions," *Time*, November 23, 2021, https://time.com/6122081/brene-brown-atlas-of-the-heart/.

One study of children ages 4–16 connected a child's ability to understand an emotion not with their developmental stage but with their language-acquisition skills.[29] Children and adults benefit when those around them grow in the vocabulary and comfort of naming and sharing their emotions.

A lot of what we learn about our emotions comes from our families of origin, but we also learn from our communities and cultures. I came into the library with my own personal experience of going to the theater. I shared it with the librarian. She gave me tools to learn more about my experience that I wouldn't likely have accessed on my own. We each share our emotions within a context, which gives us tools (and occasionally fails to give us tools) to understand our experiences with emotions.

Naming our emotions is one of those important tools. It builds emotional granularity—our ability to differentiate between emotions. The more specific I can be about what emotion I'm experiencing, the better. Our mind and internal systems process emotions more clearly when we can identify the difference between angry and irritated, excited and happy.[30] Our cultures and communities impact how we understand a certain emotion word, but the value of labeling our emotions (known as affect labeling) is still there. Labeling our emotions also helps us engage with the emotions beyond the tip of the iceberg, giving us clarity to move through our emotions without being led by them.

Fun fact: you can make up words for your emotions. We aren't restricted to only the words on a feelings wheel. Long before Urban Dictionary, people have been making up words. For example, I tend to add the suffix -ness to words to describe the way that thing impacts my emotional state. *Dailyness* is the word I use to describe the mundanity of life that can add wear and tear to certain relationships and

---

29 Simon Baron-Cohen et al., "Emotion Word Comprehension from 4 to 16 Years Old: A Developmental Survey," *Frontiers in Evolutionary Neuroscience* 2, no. 109 (November 25, 2010), https://doi.org/10.3389/fnevo.2010.00109.

30 Torre and Lieberman, "Putting Feelings into Words," 116–24.

vocations—marriage, parenting, friendship, being a student, working nine to five, and the like. I use *withness* to describe the sense of connection that comes with someone's presence in the darker or challenging moments of life. You might also use metaphors or similes for your emotions. For instance, I might say, "It feels like overripe pickles" to describe the way I've been marinating too long over someone's crummy social media post.

● ● ● ● ●

Scripture shines in the area of emotional granularity. In my research of several English translations of Scripture, I found well over two hundred emotion-related words. Emotion words and inferred emotion occur in accounts of people communicating and walking in daily life or going through deep hardship, when they are on the mountaintops or in the wilderness and desert. People in the Bible express emotion when they interact with God and with one another, when they are at work or at home, when they are arguing with or loving their neighbor, when they are trying to figure out their problems or avoid them. Emotion words and implied emotion are also attributed to God throughout Scripture.

Scripture shines in the area of emotional granularity.

Here are several examples of emotional granularity in Scripture. Note the words in bold and the specificity with which the author shares the emotional experience.

The earth **mourns** and **withers**; the world **languishes** and withers; the highest people of the earth languish. The earth lies defiled under its inhabitants; for they have transgressed the laws, violated the statutes, broken the everlasting covenant. (Isaiah 24:4–5, emphasis added)

Are they sad? Are they tired? Do they feel forgotten? Perhaps. But words like *mourn* and *languish* and even *wither* give us a much clearer picture of their experiences of grief. These words build an image; we may even feel them in our own bodies as we read.

> So if there is any **encouragement** in Christ, any **comfort** from love, any participation in the Spirit, any **affection** and **sympathy**, complete my **joy** by being of the same mind, having the same love, being in full accord and of one mind. Do nothing from **selfish ambition** or **conceit**, but in **humility** count others more significant than yourselves. (Philippians 2:1–3, emphasis added)

Paul seeks to bring his readers encouragement, not only as a mental process for hope, but also as an emotional connection. Comfort is an active emotional experience, even when wrapped around unchanging truths. Joy and humility are fruit of the Spirit apart from our sensations of them. Likewise, ambition and conceit go deeper than only feeling ambitious for a moment. Yet God gives us emotional experiences linked to these concepts as a tool of awareness. Might we be well served by noticing our feelings of selfish ambition before it becomes a character standard by which we live our lives?

Scripture offers us language for our emotions we may not find in our present culture. We'll walk through this more in part 4 on specific emotion words of the Bible.

● ● ● ● ●

My librarian proved herself to be a trusted adult who had the tools I needed to understand my experiences more fully by guiding me to a section I didn't know existed. God doesn't need to prove Himself trustworthy to us, but He does: by dying for us on the cross, by bringing us Baptism and the Lord's Supper and the Bible and the things we need to make meaning in a difficult world. God has been guiding people through their emotional experiences since creation. God experiences emotions Himself as well. Scripture makes this clear. By connecting to the Bible in our emotional experiences, we may not find an "answer" for our emotions, but we will find more language for them and a fuller sense of being seen by God in them.

It's truly wonderful how many ways God gives us to get there. God takes seriously all His promises, including the promise in Romans 8:26–27 that the Holy Spirit intercedes with groans when we have no words to express ourselves. We might try articulating our emotions in any of the following ways found throughout Scripture:

talk	grumble	wail
groan	plead	rejoice
vow	shout	sigh
cry out	complain	request

These forms of articulation help us to incorporate our emotion to better understand our own stories and to help others understand theirs. As inconvenient as they may be, our emotions have a lot to tell us. God used words to make up the Word to share His story with us. There is something, then, in giving words to all the parts of our lives and stories that connects us to Him. With His Word and the Holy Spirit, our emotions actively help us piece together the ways we experience brokenness and life and redemption.

When we ignore emotion's presence in our lives and stories—and in God's life and story—we get half-truths about God and ourselves. We conveniently avoid confessing what lies deeper by looking only at the surface. We stuff our emotions down. We stuff the truths connected to them down. As we keep burying them, these pieces of ourselves become more and more painful to look at. We "turtle," hiding in our metaphoric shells, keeping things to ourselves and even from ourselves in shame.

We can also end up hurting others when we bury our emotions. They may spew out onto those we love the most—or onto the nearest customer service agent. When we don't give them some space in our stories, emotions can boil over when we least expect it, making themselves known in outbursts or words we wish we could put back inside. In addition to stuffing down or spewing out, emotional researcher Susan David adds brooding to the list of ways we avoid emotions. She describes brooding on emotions as "endlessly stirring the pot."[31] By brooding, we might be honest about the emotions we're feeling, but we struggle to see them realistically within our story. We choose a component of our emotions to focus on or an emotion of the past that we can't let go. We miss seeing the redemption and restoration of our experiences and emotions because we hold so tightly to the brokenness of these experiences and emotions. Stuffing, spewing, and brooding are all forms of dysregulation.

● ● ● ● ●

F. Scott Spencer, in his book *Passions of the Christ: The Emotional Life of Jesus in the Gospels*, notes that God approaches His own emotions in an openhearted manner, even when they are most challenging. The author points out God's ability to move between the delight and pleasure of creating humankind in Genesis 1 to the brokenheartedness, grief, and regret of Genesis 6 while remaining true to the perfection of His divinity. Genesis 6:6 says that God "regretted that He had made man on the earth, and it grieved Him to His heart." Spencer writes: "The term for 'be sorry/regret' (naham), in the form used here, means 'allow [oneself] to be sorry' or 'allow [oneself] a change of heart regarding' a person or situation."[32]

---

31 Susan David, *Emotional Agility* (New York: Penguin, 2016), 49.

32 F. Scott Spencer, *Passions of the Christ: The Emotional Life of Jesus in the Gospels* (Grand Rapids, MI: Baker Academic, 2021), 27.

God can allow a change of heart, the ebb and flow of an emotional life, within His own being and in the story of His relationship with humankind. As He brings judgment, redemption, and restoration to humankind, He feels deeply. He allows Himself to be informed by those emotions while remaining an unchanging God. God is both perfect Law and perfect Gospel held together, and we are not, but His interaction with His emotions can teach us something about our own. May we aim for the same openheartedness toward our emotions that God reveals within Himself. We can reflect on our emotions and experience the ebb and flow of them without following them blindly. We can gather information and insight, whether in the library, in our relationships, or through many other means.

● ● ● ● ●

Isn't it miraculous that God expresses and shares His emotions with us in His Word? As Psalm 8:4 puts it, "What is man that You are mindful of him, and the son of man that You care for him?"

One encouraging aspect of emotional articulation is that the words are headed somewhere. We are not alone in these emotions. We can express our emotions before God, confess and share our emotions with Him. When we articulate our emotions before God, we also articulate our vulnerability, need, and connection to God. Connecting with God in this way, through the faithful companionship of Jesus Christ, also helps us better express and share our emotions and other vulnerabilities with other people.

The narrative of Scripture makes this clear: God sees our desperate state as humans and has compassion. God does not tell the psalmists or the author of Lamentations to keep quiet. Expressing our emotions and calling them by name helps us to look at them honestly and adjust what needs adjusting. Emotional articulation encourages us to dive deeper into God's gift of emotion and opens up our relationship with Him beyond the surface.

ARTICULATION 101

Emotional articulation is expressing our experiences with emotion through verbal and nonverbal communication. Through articulation, we can

- name our emotions;
- ask questions to get to know our emotions;
- let our emotions connect to our stories and to God's bigger story.

Consider these questions:

- What different words might I use to describe this emotion?
- Where has this emotion shown up in my story?
- What information might this emotion bring to my story?

EXPLORATION

After being a fringe member for much of my childhood, from sixth through eighth grade, I started attending a weekly confirmation class at our church. When I arrived, I had a great deal of questions.

The world is not necessarily a patient or friendly place for a twelve-year-old's questions. And this twelve-year-old had *theological* questions. They required complex answers and occasionally the ability to say, "I don't know," or, "Let's look that up and see what we can find out." Plus, I was tenacious. I would get answers. I would not be ignored.

What could have been interpreted as annoying and angsty (and I'm sure was annoying and angsty at times) instead was interpreted by my pastor as a bit bold but worthy of time and energy. This is where the snacks come in.

Pastor Fraker was a master at handling my questions. When he didn't have time to address the questions I asked loudly in class, he invited me to his office for further discussion the next week. He would sit behind his giant desk, covered with open Bibles and catechisms, papers upon papers, and snacks.

I don't remember what the snacks were, but I do remember their presence as we worked through my difficult questions. God's Spirit ignited in that office when it could so easily have been only the emotional upheaval of adolescence. Among the complex answers and Cheeto-stained fingers, twelve-year-old Heidi met a God who cared about her questions and the emotions attached to them.

• • • • •

Snacks have a way of making emotionally heated discussions easier. When I was a youth director, my office was filled with Gatorade and Frito-Lays for such a time as this. When someone experiences a loss, we bring casseroles and brownies. We think food helps us process things, even if we're the farthest from hungry. We turn to the fridge or pantry for comfort food when we feel overwhelmed or overloaded.

Part of this response is because the act of eating—getting up from where we are sitting, putting ice cream in a bowl, moving the spoon to our mouth, swallowing, digesting—is a physical process. It can certainly be used as an unhealthy distraction from our emotions, but perhaps it's also a part of our body's natural inclination to process our emotions physically.

Somatic is a medical term (derived from Greek) for something that is related to the body. *Somatic* is also a term for distinguishing the physical part of the self from the mind. Yet, the two are not so easily separated. Somatically informed therapies connect the therapy client's experiences and challenges with his or her perceived body sensations related to those experiences and challenges. Somatic approaches are informed by research from neurobiology, particularly polyvagal theory. For example, Gestalt therapy proposes that by nature, trauma can leave behind unfinished work, images, emotions, or sensations that need to be processed in the body. The Gottman method of couples therapy recommends using pulse oximeters to note the moment one or both partners have a physical response to being emotionally "flooded" during a challenging discussion. When we are emotionally flooded, our body responds physically to the perceived threat: our breathing speeds up, our heart rate increases, we are prepping for action. Emotions are part of our mind and mental processes, but they are connected to our body as well. Not all our sensations are emotions, but the two are intricately linked. That connection is worthy of our attention.

● ● ● ● ●

I learned in my own therapeutic experience that giving our sensations, feelings, and emotions appropriate space is also a powerful reminder that God makes space for us when we're not at our best. The anxiety, frustration, sadness, struggle, and energy that comes from living in a broken world needs to go somewhere. We cannot hold that all inside of us. Instead, as we find appropriate ways to let our emotions manifest themselves, we learn to live in the belief that God's grace is available for all of me, all of my life, including my emotions.

Our body's natural ability, given by God, to process emotions through physical movement might be one of many reasons why exercise positively impacts our mental health. Movement has more purpose than meets the eye. Every day our bodies send gentle and not-so-gentle reminders of what they need—to eat or release tension or get some quality sleep and the emotional and memory processing that goes with it. Movement as an emotional process takes what we held inside for so long and allows our bodies to release it.

Contemplation and articulation are wonderful tools in our toolbox, but sometimes it's a challenge to put our thoughts together. Some emotions like to stay below the surface, which makes it hard to formulate words around them. Exploring our emotions with movement gives us another tool to process our emotions when that happens.

Some emotions like to stay below the surface.

How might we engage in movement-oriented emotional processing? You likely do a lot of this on your own—taking a walk after a long day's work, going for a run when the stress of life builds, or leaving the room to put some space between you and someone whom you find irritating at the moment. Eye movement desensitization and reprocessing (EMDR) therapy uses a tool called the body scan to identify emotions connected to an experience. The body scan gives the therapy client time to recognize any residual physical sensations related to the thoughts and memory they are processing. Our body responds in many ways to challenges, to people, and to things that bring us a sense of refuge or joy. But those responses are easy to miss when we are in the midst of the experience. The stillness and quiet of the body scan gives us valuable information for recognizing our emotions and finding the why and how of our experiences.

●　●　●　●　●

Just as my pastor took time with my questions, our bodies appreciate when we take time with their questions, as it were. When we engage with our physical experience of emotions, we will become more familiar with emotional arousal and valence, which are really useful for helping our physical bodies experience emotion without being overwhelmed by it.

Emotional arousal is the fancy term for the intensity of an emotion. We often don't recognize emotions until they are extremely strong or intense in our bodies. Articulating the name of an emotion and where we are feeling it in our bodies helps us start to recognize it earlier, when it is less intense. Imagine sensing playfulness or joy more often because we were aware of them even when they were small. These are often pleasant or pleasurable emotions for us, and so we would enjoy more of that pleasure. In the same way, imagine being aware of our sadness before we feel overwhelmed by it. Imagine being aware of our anger before it is pointed in someone's direction with disdain.

Emotional valence is the sense of whether we like an emotion, our pleasure or discomfort with it. Valence includes the positive or negative attributions we give to any emotion. Valence tends to have a lot of cultural and familial baggage as well, which makes it harder for us to work through. It's easy to assume that if we find an emotion pleasant or uncomfortable, God feels the same. I would heavily caution against assumptions about how God views emotion and instead encourage learning what God says about Himself through Scripture. Getting to know God better is always a good approach when we have complex questions and assumptions.

● ● ● ● ●

In preparation for writing this book, I spent a year reading the Bible for its emotional content. Rather, first, I put off reading the Bible for its emotional content. How presumptive of me was it to ask God to show me emotions in the Bible? Dismantling my assumptions about emotions by looking for emotion seemed circular at best. And God is not a genie. It isn't necessarily healthy when we interact with Him simply to get what we want out of Him. When the Holy Spirit wouldn't leave me alone, I put my assumptions on the table before God. Then I opened my Bible and started by reading the books of the Bible I expected to have the most emotion words or expressions of emotion. I finished with the books I thought might be the least emotionally charged. As you may have guessed, I was wrong, which is a good place of humility to find yourself in during the research process.

A surprising amount of the emotions in the Bible are experienced physically rather than verbalized—more bones wasting, hearts yearning, shouts of rejoicing, peals of laughter, and the like than I expected. One explanation is that somatic manifestations were readily accepted and encouraged in the Hebrew culture. Wailing was an expected rather than uncomfortable part of the mourning process. Vibrant songs and shouts of joy were just as important a part of the feasts and festivals of temple worship as readings and moments of silence for confession are today. The Bible is, among other things, a telling of the human experience before God and in relationship with God. The amount of physical expression of emotions in Scripture reveals what current research confirms: we experience emotions *in the body,* and therefore movement *of the body* can be helpful for emotional processing.

The Bible offers us lots of suggestions for physical movement and exploration. Some are more creative, but many are simple and easy to incorporate.

- **Lift up your head**
  - Psalm 24:7–10; Genesis 40:12–14
  - Move your head to a forward-facing or upward-facing position, the opposite of a position of shame or humiliation. You might be surprised by how often you find yourself looking down.
- **Rise up**
  - Micah 7:8; Ezra 10:4
  - Stand up from a seated position. This movement gives a sense of the empowerment and capability God brings to us when our emotions and experiences leave us feeling powerless or incapable.
- **Spread out/lift up your hands**
  - Psalm 143:1–6; 1 Timothy 2:1–8
  - Hold your hands out or up to God and offer the weights and the joys before Him.
- **Weep**
  - 1 Samuel 30:1–4; Romans 12:15
  - Yes, crying! Do it! Weeping also includes other movements, such as putting your hands to your face or

connecting your upper torso with your lower body in some way.

- **Grind or gnash teeth**
  - Job 16:9; Acts 7:54
  - This is a biblical expression of anger or rage. It's also a reminder of the massive amounts of emotional tension we hold in our jaw and teeth. Try tightening and releasing the tension in your jaw and teeth, particularly when you are upset, but also preventatively throughout the day.

- **Bow**
  - Psalm 95:1–6; Romans 14:10–12
  - Bowing is intended for God and really no other. Bowing gives us a physical way to recognize our place of smallness before God, which can be strangely reassuring.

- **Dance**
  - 2 Samuel 6:13–15; Jeremiah 31:13
  - There is something refreshing in recognizing the freedom of God's provision for us in Christ by dancing like David danced or remembering that joy does come in its time.

- **Go up**
  - Psalm 122; Luke 2:33–38
  - Like the Israelites going up to the temple for feasts, changing our location can help our brains switch gears. Try going to a different room, outside, or to an entirely different place. Connecting the dots that God

is with us in each place reminds us of God's grace and presence in our lives.

These other movements might also be useful:

stretching	pulling on a rope
doing a pushup against the wall	punching a pillow or bag
putting your hands in sand or dirt	tearing up paper
coloring an intricate design/picture	pressing and feeling both feet against the floor

The goal of processing emotions with movement is not to give emotion all our time and energy or to overspiritualize every detail of our day. Instead, we want to be creative in recognizing the many ways God has designed us for restoration—for life, not for death—even in a broken world. Christ's salvation is at work in our emotional lives. When Christ died and rose to save us, that redemptive mission had ripple effects, some of which we'll only see and understand in the new creation. I am endlessly amazed at the many ways God's grace comes into our lives. As the writer of Ephesians reminds us,

Now to Him who is able to do far more abundantly than all that we ask or think, according to the power at work within us, to Him be glory in the church and in Christ Jesus throughout all generations, forever and ever. Amen. (3:20–21)

EXPLORATION 101

Emotional exploration is acknowledging the physical aspects of emotional processing and giving our bodies space to express emotions, named and unnamed. Through exploration, we can

- identify emotions in the body;
- consider our corporeal pleasure or discomfort with our emotions;
- use intentional movement to process emotions physically.

Consider these questions:

- Where do I feel this emotion in my body?
- Do I like this emotion or does it make me uncomfortable?
- Why might I connect pleasure or discomfort with this emotion?

CONNECTION

There are moments when crying in the bathroom is the best option. I encountered one such moment my freshman year of high school. Most of us can relate to the feeling of emotional overwhelm: the emotions are building inside, one comment throws us over the edge, and suddenly the emotions are dying to get out. Embarrassing myself in the middle of the high school cafeteria would have been the buttercream frosting on top of the layer cake of emotions.

Instead, I chose the first stall of the women's bathroom as a safe haven to gather myself (read: to have a sobfest). Eventually I heard a soft tap on the stall door and a voice gently asking, "Is there anything I can do to help?"

Did I want help? Dare I open the door? Who was asking? Would they judge me for all the snot? Did they know what happened? Would I have to explain the whole situation? Why were they being so nice? My need for someone to be *with* me in this moment overrode each of those questions. I opened the stall door slowly and said, "I'm just sad. It's been a rotten day."

To which the mystery high school bathroom companion replied, "We've all been there."

I took a deep breath. I said thank you. A minute later I washed my hands and walked back out into the cafeteria, feeling ready for whatever life threw at me next.

Would you look at that? Emotions successfully processed.

●　●　●　●　●

In Western culture, we most often think of emotional processing as an *intra*personal experience, meaning between me, myself, and I. We might expand that as Christians to me, myself, and God. Because of this cultural vantage point, the last three sections of this book may have sounded like this:

Contemplation—I can think about my emotions on my own.

Articulation—I can name my emotions on my own (and I probably prefer it that way).

Exploration—I can move from one space to another. I can take a moment if I need a moment.

Sometimes being on our own is better than, say, in a crowded cafeteria. And it's true that much of the work of processing emotions in my life is up to me. No one else can feel the sensations in my body, and no one else can choose to notice them rather than sideline or bury them. But it's also true that emotions are relational experiences as much as personal ones—something we don't like to admit in Western culture. However, there is great value in processing our emotions through *inter*personal experience, or *between people.* Cultures that are more community oriented understand this a little more intuitively.

We are each impacted emotionally by our families and friends, our communities, and world events. We are impacted emotionally by God's presence, or God's seeming absence, in our lives. Our emotions come from inside of us, but they are very often formed through our connections, which makes them good candidates for being processed in connection.

Emotional processing through connection means processing our emotions through the act of being with or traveling alongside another person. Some people will travel life together for a moment, like the girl who helped me in the bathroom, and others for a lifetime. Processing our emotions through connection is not done simply by filling the same space, like on a commuter train or in a room full of bodies at a party.

Rather, emotional processing through connection means intentionally choosing to be with the other person, to be present and available, in a moment of emotion—what I call *withness.* This occurs more than just in moments of emotional overwhelm. We can also talk with those in our lives about the topic of emotion, which is its own form of processing. Emotional processing through connection requires that one or both parties are comfortable with acknowledging, talking about, and feeling their emotions to some degree. It probably also requires one or both parties to work against their personal discomfort around certain emotions.

Sitting beside people in their emotion or allowing them to share about their emotion says to them, "There's space for that here. There's space for you here." Through this connection, we send the message that they're welcome to process that emotion at a deeper level. Many people feel like the world lacks space for them. They may have room to move and breathe and all that, yet it still feels like the world refuses to make space for their eccentricities, their needs, their big emotions.

God continuously says to us, "There's space for that here. There's space for you here." He says it actively in His Word. He said it loudest in sending His Son to die for us on the cross to bring forgiveness and to repair our relationship. God also says it in Baptism, in the Lord's Supper, in the creation He gave us to care for and enjoy, in creating concepts like community and connection, in bringing hope for our despair, and in bringing joy for our victories. Sometimes God's work and *withness* can be hard to see, so He provides us a vivid reminder of *withness* every day: one another.

God continuously says to us, "There's space for that here. There's space for you here."

It is so tempting to withdraw from connection, whether human or divine. We have all had experiences of someone dropping our emotions on the floor when we were vulnerable enough to share them. We each have felt alone and been alone. Most of us have felt embarrassment or humiliation as the result of a display of emotion. Some of us didn't grow up in an environment that valued *withness*. But God says, "I will never leave you or forsake you" (Deuteronomy 31:6). God doesn't reject or embarrass or leave us to be all alone, even when the *feeling* of emptiness lives inside of us. God says, "There is space for that here. There's space for you here." Loneliness and its related emotions are signs sent by our psyches that we were made for relationship. When we feel like withdrawing, connection is the emotional processing component we need most.

● ● ● ● ●

Self-regulation is one kind of emotional regulation or processing. Self-regulation is a person's awareness of their internal workings, particularly their own thoughts and feelings, and their ability to engage with them in a way that supports health. We need an awareness inside of us that recognizes stuffing and spewing and brooding when we try them on. Self-regulation tools like contemplation, articulation, and exploration help us become aware of our thoughts and feelings and consider our perceptions within context to check for accuracy.

Co-regulation is another important type of emotional regulation. In fact, self-regulation skills originate from our early co-regulation experiences, and co-regulation can help support us when self-regulation disappoints. The term *co-regulation* originally described adult support of an infant in development, but now it is applied to caring relationships of many ages. The Duke Center for Child and Family Policy explains co-regulation as "the supportive process between caring adults and children, youth, or young adults that *fosters* self-regulation development" (emphasis added).[33] We think we can go it alone, but we were made for relationship.

Crying in the bathroom is an option in this life but thank goodness for those people who say, "I don't want someone to have to cry alone." Thank goodness for people who shine the light of God's love by stepping into their neighbor's world for a second to offer co-regulation, often without realizing what they are doing.

Relationships that co-regulate with us are usually found in our families and closest friendships, but it's not limited to those. God is always working between people in ways we cannot see. Emotional processing might happen with teachers, classmates, mentors, neighbors, co-workers, health care professionals, librarians, store clerks, and more. Co-regulation is a neurobiological reality of God's design for humankind to love our neighbor as ourselves.

Co-regulation is about responsiveness. Co-regulation is supported by warm and caring environments that make space for our emotions and also boundaries for what we do with those emotions. Responsiveness doesn't necessarily mean "doing" in a relationship. It also includes the act of being in relationship—showing up, checking in, making space, sitting alongside, and validating while offering boundaries, especially when life and emotions get uncomfortable.

● ● ● ● ●

Sometimes we are so good at connecting with other people and their emotions that we forget the boundaries part of co-regulation. We can better engage in connection as an emotional process when we're

---

33 K. D. Rosenbalm and D. W. Murray, "Caregiver Co-Regulation across Development: A Practice Brief" (OPRE Brief #2017-80), Office of Planning, Research, and Evaluation, Administration for Children and Families, U.S. Department of Health and Human Services, January 5, 2018, https://www.acf.hhs.gov/opre/report /co-regulation-birth-through-young-adulthood-practice-brief.

aware of transference. Transference is a psychological phenomenon in which one person shifts the emotions they are experiencing or that are meant for another person onto a different person. This might look like being mad at my mom and subconsciously creating reasons to be mad at my therapist, or the close friend, sitting across from me.

Transference is closely related to some of the defense mechanisms identified earlier. When an emotion is uncomfortable for us, we may project it or displace it in an attempt to disconnect from it. Projection is when we assume others have the emotion we ourselves are having. For example, if I'm anxious, I may interpret the person across from me as being anxious. If that person doesn't have the awareness to set a boundary, maybe they do pick up my anxiety. Now we pass the anxiety back and forth, stuck in a tennis match we didn't mean to sign up for. This bouncing ball of anxiety weasels its way into so many relationships and rooms, tossed from person to person. We may also displace the emotions we feel about one person toward another person entirely because it feels safer or less unpleasant.

Transference, projection, and displacement are subconscious actions that serves us, but they don't usually serve us well. These emotional negotiations often start because they seem to keep us safe or help us in some way at a specific time. They also serve what theologians and pastors refer to as "the old Adam." Romans 3:23–24 talks about the parts of us that lean toward sin and unhealth. That unhealthy inclination wants to avoid the truth of our brokenness and will use all those other defense mechanisms to escape it. Sometimes we wrap others into these defenses too. Transference has little to do with negative intent. Most often, it comes from a lack of awareness and reveals once again that we cannot get ourselves to health on our own. We are humans loved by our great God and in need of God's grace in Jesus Christ, in our aloneness and our connectedness.

We tend to hold a lot of shame when we feel most alone.

● ● ● ● ●

Our need for grace is one reason emotional processing through connection is especially healing. Let's go back to high school Heidi in a bathroom stall. We tend to hold a lot of shame when we feel most alone, in those moments when we find a bathroom a better companion than a room swarming with people. We are all too aware of our faults when emotions overwhelm, even when they have little to do with the moment at hand. Connectedness reminds us that we are more than our faults or embarrassments and that God sees us even when we feel lost in the mire of brokenness. Another human asking "Is there any way I can help?" is not the same as God speaking through His Word, but those moments of connection can lead us back to God's Word to hear and find the truth, rather than shut Him out. God is more believable in our connectedness. The Body of Christ—the people God has brought together in Jesus—has much to offer here. We need one another in more ways than we know. We were made for community, and when our faith communities hold space for our emotions with God's grace and truth at the center, we each benefit.

The Bible offers many examples of processing emotions through connection:

trust (Jeremiah 17:7–8)	hold fast (Hebrews 10:19–25)
companionship (2 Kings 2)	comfort (2 Corinthians 1:3–5)
friendship (1 Samuel 18:1–5)	shade/rest (Jonah 4)
listen/give ear (Psalm 5:1–3)	pour out (Lamentations 2:11–12)
praise (Exodus 15:1–18)	encourage (Acts 15:30–32)
bear with one another (Colossians 3:12–14)	stir up (2 Peter 1:3–15)

Some of those options involve sitting alongside someone. Others include active communication with God or other people. One of the most direct forms of emotional processing through connection is offering. Offering means opening ourselves up to be known by God, to be vulnerable before Him. Since we are already seen and known by God without our own effort, we could leave it at that, but the act of offering engages our awareness of our vulnerability for co-regulation.

Being vulnerable with God or other people tends to push all our emotion buttons. In this way, vulnerability opens us up for more-thorough emotional processing. Vulnerability brings those under-the-surface emotions into the open, so the processing goes deeper. To do this, though, we need to feel safe. Vulnerability and boundaries go hand in hand. We can read our environment and the relationships within it to determine which will serve us at that moment, vulnerability or boundaries (or a combination of both). Take my experience in high school: The cafeteria sounded loud, a thousand conversations of people wrapped up in their own drama. I had witnessed or experienced interactions in the cafeteria that led me to believe it was not a friendly place for leaky emotions. In that instance, I led with boundaries but found a place for my vulnerability. Thankfully, someone else led with vulnerability and was willing to step into my emotional experience with me, in a private place, with an offer of grace.

We don't have to share with all people all the time. Some people will make us uncomfortable or, worse, bring shame into our lives. We can take comfort in and note of the way God leads us, including with emotions. God requires nothing of us beyond Jesus Christ crucified and risen. God never pushes Himself on us. God continuously stands in our lives, offering help and guidance, not peddling advice and requirements. This is a balm for our emotions. May we offer the same to those in our midst: "Is there anything I can do to help?" Sometimes the answer will be no; there will be times for vulnerability and times for boundaries. Grace is a gift, not a mandate.

God requires nothing of us beyond Jesus Christ crucified and risen.

Offering can be as simple as a breath prayer: breathing in, "God, I am overwhelmed by life, and I have many emotions inside of me," and breathing out, "Jesus, You are in all things and You understand all things, including my emotions."

Offering might also look like a fuller conversation with God. God has emotions toward us too. God is delighted by us. We make Him angry sometimes. God has empathy toward us and also boundaries with us. Being in active relationship with God each day gives us fundamental grounding, knowing there is a place we can always turn, a place where our emotions never lead us to shame because of Jesus Christ.

God also brings other people into our lives to share with, to talk to, to process life and its gunk. There is vulnerability in this too, but with God between us, we can share more than we thought and see which boundaries might be necessary and when. Intentionally processing our emotions through connection also allows us to process the stuff of this life, the good and wonderful alongside the challenging. The invitation to connect may remain between us and God, acknowledging His presence to see the grace and mercy of Jesus Christ in every emotion. Sometimes that connection expands to other intimate relationships that offer spaces of unique safety and assurance over the journey of our lives. And other times, that connection comes for a moment in odd or modest spaces, like a bathroom outside a high school cafeteria.

CONNECTION 101

Emotional connection is intentionally connecting to God and other people as emotional beings or processing our emotions through the act of being with another person. Through connection, we can

- acknowledge the emotions "in the room";
- acknowledge the impact of emotions between people;
- share both empathy and boundaries in relationship with others.

Consider these questions:

- Who can help me understand this emotion?
- Who can help me hold this emotion gently?
- What boundaries do I need to connect with God in my emotions?
- What boundaries do I need to help me connect with another person in my emotions?

PART 4
Specific Emotions

FORGOTTEN EMOTIONS OF SCRIPTURE

In my family growing up, therapy meant many things, but it especially meant good burgers.

While I was in middle school, my parents committed us to family therapy every other week or so. Each visit, we arrived at an office with flowered couches, dated floor lamps, and one of the kindest, most insightful women I have ever met. After therapy came burger time—not skimpy burgers either, but big, juicy burger heaven at Fuddruckers.

At Fuddruckers, I stepped up to the glass and picked out my burger like people pick out their lobster at fancy seafood restaurants. There were baskets of fries with special seasoning and tall glasses of name-brand cola.

Fuddruckers was the perfect post-therapy huddle because there was no pretension. Being able to sit around a table and eat yummy food and reflect or simply laugh made therapy much less intimidating. Our burger stops lifted the shame that can come with going to therapy for the first time, making something that once felt big and isolating eventually feel normal and connecting.

●　●　●　●　●

Developmentally, children and adolescents are naturally egocentric, meaning that they think of things in relationship to themselves first. This natural, very human characteristic helps them maintain resilience in a challenging world and keep growing into adulthood. The problem that comes with this natural attention to self is that children tend to also carry the weight of adult problems on their own shoulders. Therapy is a good place to sort through these things, whether as a child or an adult. But sorting is intimidating and can feel scary. When we don't have words to describe the pain inside of us, how in the world will we explain it to the kind lady on her flowered couch?

We often need something like Fuddruckers, something that provides a bit of hope alongside whatever is intimidating or scary. Fuddruckers made therapy days special, which lowered the level of intimidation for the whole experience. The healing that came from the joy and excitement of our burger stop eventually became more about therapy and less about burgers. Sometimes we need a link like burgers or tacos or iced coffee or something else less intimidating to get us to the things we need, like therapy.

● ● ● ● ●

The purpose of this book is to give you a foundation that creates a link between your emotions and the God of the universe. I also wanted to make sorting through the concept of emotions and our emotional selves less intimidating. Nothing is quite as intimidating in a Christian conversation about emotions as people's opinions about the emotion words we find in the Bible. *Joy, fear, hate, justice*—these words and others carry cultural baggage and whatever ideas we each associate with them. I have noticed that in Christian circles, we tend to elevate the emotion words our culture values, as if God must also value them.

I propose we take this chance to widen our view—to discover the more unfamiliar emotion words of the Bible and look beyond the emotions we find frequently in our culture or value alongside our culture. In the way burgers helped me begin to find the words I needed in therapy, I pray these "forgotten" emotion words of Scripture add insight to your emotional vocabulary and release a little of that cultural baggage. These words, which are not used often in Western culture, have their own value. Expanding our vocabulary with the varied emotions that the Bible recognizes as part of the human experience makes conversations around our emotions more hope filled, less intimidating.

In the Bible, we see God value what our culture often does not; we see real people, real problems, real solutions, and very real emotion. The Bible is active and life-giving truth. It tells us who we are in Christ Jesus, our Savior, and who we are becoming through our relationship with Him. The Bible is also humanity's story, a collection of writings from complicated people to other complicated people.

In the Bible, we see God value what our culture often does not.

This most important and life-giving book and the unfamiliar emotion words taken from it provide incredible insight into the emotional life of God and our own emotional lives. It offers the comfort of connectedness with God, with the believers who have gone before us with their own emotional turmoil and baggage, and with Jesus, our Redeemer and Lord, who experienced His own emotions. The Bible gives words, exploration, movement, and connection to emotional experiences.

The Bible is not always emotive. Scripture is selective in its descriptions based on the Holy Spirit's inspiration and each human writer's style. God's emotions aren't all there is to Him, nor are emotions all there is to the people we find in biblical accounts. It's important that we not add more than what the Bible expressly says about the emotions in the following sections. For instance, when we encounter the anger of God, it's easy to see an angry God. When we encounter the delight of God, it's easy to see a delighted God. But God will not be cherry-picked. Emotions in Scripture don't necessarily come with a systematic theology to them. We hold together both what is revealed to us and what remains hidden from us. We can be comforted by God's fullness, rather than reduce Him to the simplicity we crave.

● ● ● ● ●

One of the best examples of a forgotten emotion word in Scripture is the term _desolate_ or *desolation*. Some form of this word appears in the ESV translation of the Bible over 130 times. The concept is prevalent in the Hebrew Scriptures before the birth of Jesus Christ, yet we also see the experience of desolation in the Greek Scriptures of the Gospels and the Early Church. Feeling desolate speaks of life's devastations. Desolation recognizes the universal yet unique experiences of humans as they bear witness to horrific things in their time and place. Feeling desolate and calling it by name is the honest expression of times when life feels more like a wasteland and less like abundance and living water.

Those experiencing desolation often feel forgotten by God. To complicate it, when we look closer at desolation in the Bible, it seems these wasteland moments might be attributed to the actions of God. How does this God fit with the one whom we call good? In this way, desolation is an emotional experience that brings up theological questions and struggles. Job 16:6–8 speaks strongly to the emotional experience of feeling abandoned, rejected, and desolate:

> If I speak, my pain is not assuaged, and if I forbear, how much of it leaves me? Surely now God has worn me out; He has made desolate all my company. And He has shriveled me up, which is a witness against me, and my leanness has risen up against me; it testifies to my face.

Having a word for the sense of forgottenness that comes with desolation helps us cling to God through our questions and struggles.

Words like *desolate* and *desolation* give us language for the pain and frustration and sorrow that come with wondering if God still sees us or cares about us. The word *desolation* and our encounters with it in Scripture offer some validation for our experiences of feeling like God is absent. In providing spiritual care in these circumstances, I've noticed that the ability to speak these emotions and thoughts aloud keeps people connected to God, not their ability to avoid these emotions or maintain a "right" or "proper" perception of God and His presence. Life in a broken world will always have its desolations, and we each will feel desolate at times. The Bible acknowledges that reality and gives us the words to name those feelings.

●　●　●　●　●

Jesus came into this world. Jesus died and rose for this world. Jesus is coming back for this world so that desolation and our experiences of desolation are not the end of our story, so that forgottenness is not what defines us. Christ Jesus came to save sinners. He also came to save the forgotten ones, the desolate ones, the petulant ones, the indignant ones, the contemptuous ones, the delighted ones, and the weary ones.

In these last chapters, we'll look at our emotions through other words and language we use less often or might have forgotten. We'll ask questions about the context of these words within the Bible. And we'll watch as the Holy Spirit works through God's Word to faithfully bring Christ's truth and grace to our lives.

We will only be able to skim the surface of emotions in Scripture in this section. The term *Christocentric*, which means "centered on Christ," describes the main purpose of Scripture: that God reveals His heart, plan, will, and all things through Jesus (Colossians 1:24–29). Jesus is the point of every verse and every page. I encourage you to dig into the Bible long after you've finished this book and continue to look for the redeeming work of Jesus across the pages of Scripture and in your emotional life. And don't forget to include your version of a therapy burger. When the work is difficult or intimidating, try a comforting link like a snack, beverage, or friendly conversation to make it easier to approach the Bible and God's deep affection for you.

God does not leave us in our light or darkness. No emotion is outside His reach. When my parents took me to therapy and out for burgers, they conveyed to me, "We see you. You are not forgotten." I pray the rest of this book reminds you that while some words may no longer be familiar to us, forgotten by our culture and time, we are never forgotten by God in Jesus Christ.

DELIGHT

My childhood best friend, Julie, and I were inseparable. Every winter, we went sledding down the hill that made up her front lawn. Every summer, we swung on the swings of my swing set until we made make the rickety bottom jump out of the ground. We giggled late into the night and through many daylight hours too.

My strongest memories with Julie are of times in her living room, chairs pushed aside to make ample room for our invisible stage. We danced, sang, and choreographed our own versions of Madonna's "La Isla Bonita," Prince's "1999," and Cyndi Lauper's "Girls Just Wanna Have Fun." There were side ponytails and leotards, leggings and legwarmers. We were nothing if not serious about our musical endeavors.

Julie and I regularly practiced what we considered our masterpiece: a musical rendition of the life of Davy Crockett. I believe our deep commitment to this piece had mostly to do with the fact that we had procured both the sheet music and a tape of background instrumentals with which to carry out our two-woman show. We argued over rewrites, considered staging, and snacked on apples and peanut butter with pencils tucked behind our ears.

● ● ● ● ●

These afternoons with Julie were full of delight. The experience of two nine-year-old girls united in friendship, laughing, singing, eating, talking, and dancing aptly portrays two indicators of delight we find in Scripture: relationship and wholeheartedness. These two indicators set delight apart from other pleasure-filled emotions like joy, happiness, satisfaction, and contentment.

First, those afternoons were more about relationship than they were about what we produced with our time together. The goal of delight isn't really the Broadway production but the relationships that form and strengthen in the work of it.

Second, those afternoons demanded our whole selves, and we gave them gladly. There are many areas of life where we hold portions of ourselves back. Julie and I were all-in during our time together. We did not just sit around and think about music. I can't remember a time one of us stopped dancing for the embarrassment of it all. When a relationship is deep enough and safe enough, we experience moments we want to enter into with our heart, soul, mind, and strength.

Delight is an active experience of relationship and wholeheartedness, not a passive, cognitive idea. When we delight, we feel the connection. We feel the moment because we are all-in, completely involved, in a way we usually aren't or can't be. At Jesus' Baptism in Luke 3, God says He is well pleased, or delighted, with His Son. God is wholeheartedly present in this event quite clearly as the Trinity— Jesus the Son, the Spirit in the form of a dove, and the Father's voice. The world sees in this single moment that the three-in-one God is connected in all things, forming a circle of delight, of mutuality and joy.

We are not God as Jesus Christ is, but we are grafted into the pleasure of God and the delight of God through our relationship with Jesus. God calls Jesus His "beloved" Son at His Baptism. This is not an accidental word choice.[34] The name "beloved" hearkens back to the reciprocity and delight the Jewish followers of God would have heard again and again in the poetry of the Song of Songs. Delight

---

34   Arthur A. Just, *Luke 1:1–9:50*, Concordia Commentary (St. Louis, MO: Concordia Publishing House, 1996), 160–62.

flows back and forth between the two lovers of the Song, a two-way street of mutuality:

> As an apple tree among the trees of the forest, so is my beloved among the young men. With great delight I sat in his shadow, and his fruit was sweet to my taste. (Song of Songs 2:3)
>
> How beautiful and pleasant you are, O loved one, with all your delights! (Song of Songs 7:6)

If it seems odd to you that God would use the relationship of two lovers to point us to Jesus or help us understand God's relationship with His people, you would not be in the minority. When people read *Altogether Beautiful*, my study of the Song of Songs, they often tell me, "I had no idea there was so much about Jesus in there!" It is the intimacy of the poem or song that makes it remarkably delightful. The culture and language in which the Song of Songs was written was much more comfortable with intimacy than our modern culture is. And God chose that time, place, culture, and language to convey His message, as He did for all of Scripture.

Intimacy is the power source for relationship and wholeheartedness, the two necessary components of delight. Think of all the time and energy Julie and I put into our performances. Those were also hours of work growing our relationship together. Intimacy *is* work. In our relationship with God, we get to experience delight upon delight because Jesus did the work and sent the Spirit to work in us. And we are active participants in faith, not spectators, through our relationship with Jesus. Delight comes not only in the existence of the relationship but also in the daily, wholehearted effort of that relationship.

●　●　●　●　●

The Psalms speak of delight more than any other book of the Bible. In the Psalms, we see people delighting in the Law of God, or what is written by God, and in the active work of God in their lives. The psalmists tell their stories of crying and hurting, singing and dancing with God alongside them:

> Blessed is the man who walks not in the counsel of the wicked, nor stands in the way of sinners, nor sits in the seat of scoffers; but his delight is in the law of the LORD, and on His law he meditates day and night. (Psalm 1:1–2)
>
> Let those who delight in My righteousness shout for joy and be glad and say evermore, "Great is the LORD, who delights in the welfare of His servant!" (Psalm 35:27)
> In the way of Your testimonies I delight as much as in all riches. (Psalm 119:14)

Delight feeds our connection with God rather than feeding the emotion itself. Emotions of pleasure can leave us wanting more of that emotion when they were intended to lead us to want more of God. It's easy to get confused and replace the Giver with the gift. When we reclaim the forgotten emotion of delight and call it by its biblical name, it can point us to God. Maybe delight is more likely to help us see God than other emotions of pleasure because of its mutuality. When we experience delight, we're delighted with someone or something—in marriage or in friendship or with God's creation. We experience delight before God and with God.

We experience delight before God and with God.

What about when a relationship doesn't hold delight? What about when my relationship with God doesn't delight? As always, it's an important part of our all-around health to see our emotions as momentary experiences that serve a purpose for their time, giving us information for the moment. Emotions do not solidify or validate a relationship; therefore, delight does not solidify or validate a relationship. The validity of delight happens the other way around: relationship makes delight. If it's not relationship oriented, it's not delight. The emotion is dependent on the relationship; the relationship is not dependent on the emotion. Relationship is what sustains us, the broader thing that is always present even when the emotions are not.

Can we make delight about us? You betcha. Are there people in Scripture who delight in fruit they shouldn't pick from trees and sexuality outside what has been given to them? Yes. Humans mess up delight just as we mess up any emotion or experience. Yet, delight is not a selfish "look at me!" kind of emotion by nature. Just like any emotion, we can elevate it beyond its place as an informant in our lives. In that way, it's wise to take delight as it comes in our relationship with God and with others, not try to manufacture it wherever we can get it. Delight is one emotion we experience in relationship, but it's not the goal of relationship.

● ● ● ● ●

When Jesus comes again, delight will abound. On that day our tears will be wiped away, and we will live fully in the delight of God. We will live fully in relationship with God in the new heaven and new earth. We see a foretaste of this delight and joy in the vineyards and gardens of Scripture from Genesis to Song of Songs to John 10. In the here and now, we only experience delight in snatches. Our delight is coupled with longing for that day ahead. When you long for delight, listen to the stories of those touched by Jesus and let yourself be delighted. Snap a picture of the sunset and before you share it with friends on the internet, participate in a moment of delight by marveling at God's creativity. Look in the mirror and know that God looks on His people with delight, even if we're feeling the pangs of desolation or longing:

> You shall be a crown of beauty in the hand of the LORD,
> and a royal diadem in the hand of your God. You shall no
> more be termed Forsaken, and your land shall no more
> be termed Desolate, but you shall be called My Delight Is
> in Her, and your land Married; for the LORD delights in
> you, and your land shall be married. For as a young man
> marries a young woman, so shall your sons marry you,
> and as the bridegroom rejoices over the bride, so shall
> your God rejoice over you. (Isaiah 62:3–5)

The emotion of delight reminds us we are not alone. In this world, we need that reminder of our connection with God. The next time you notice something good, especially something beloved, try the phrase "Well, that's delightful!" and recognize the Maker of all delights as He walks among your days.

NOTICE AND NAME DELIGHT

- What gifts around you do you find delightful?
- What aspects of your relationship with God bring delight into your life?
- What does delight feel like and look like to you?

Related words: joy, gladness, pleased, satisfied, longing, exult, content, jubilant, pleasant, thrilled, merry, mirth, playful, desire, amazed, marvel, awe, curiosity, treasure up

DISTRESS

We all have moments in life we would pay good money not to relive. Mine is the day we almost lost our daughter Jyeva.

Jyeva is strong and creative. She loves hockey and hiking and knows how to keep a good beat on her drum set. When she was five, we lived briefly in Haiti. In a perfect storm, Jyeva contracted typhoid and malaria and had an allergic reaction to her antibiotics all at once. At three in the morning, we drove down a mountain to fly to Fort Lauderdale for further treatment.

When the plane landed in Florida, Jyeva was suddenly unresponsive. I tried to pick her up and couldn't. As the plane emptied around us, I begged for help. No one stopped. I was alone. I was tired. I was scared.

I could feel my pulse speed up. I was shaking. My hands were white and clammy. As the flight attendant came toward me, my words came out loud and desperate: "Please help me. Why will no one help? My daughter is sick. She can't walk. I can't move her. HELP!" I clenched my fists and stomped my feet, unable to monitor, much less regulate, my anger, fear, sadness. I was in distress.

Thank goodness for compassion. The next moments were a blur of action: soothing words from the flight attendant, the kindness and tenacity of an airline employee with a wheelchair, a 911 call, and leaving the airport in an ambulance on the same tarmac we came in on. With the help of strangers, we were on our way to healing.

Distress is scary, exhausting, and overwhelming. But it becomes manageable when touched by the love, mercy, and gentleness of God and those around us.

●　●　●　●　●

Distress encapsulates the moments of life when our emotions are heightened beyond what we can mentally and/or physically tolerate, and it's a whole-person experience. When we're overloaded in distress, our bodies react. Our breathing gets quicker and heart rate increases. We might become fidgety or tense. We might suddenly need to move around or change locations. We might also check out, our bodies shutting down like a computer—confused, overheated, unable to function. In distress, our minds often become overloaded as well. There are too many thoughts to hang on to about the thing before us. Sometimes irrational ideas or nonsense words go off like fireworks in our brain. Questions rise, rapid fire: "Why? Why me? Why this? Why now?" These questions may last only for a moment as answers also rise to the surface, long-tucked-away promises becoming relevant and real in new ways. Our questions also may break through those promises and linger much longer. There is no shame in the questions. Life is heavy, and distress upends us, no matter the strength of our spirit.

When we experience distress, the situation that causes it may not be life or death, as it was with my daughter, but it will be marked by extremes. Distress pushes us over the edge, sending us tumbling from the crest of a mountain. The topple can take us by surprise, happening in a flash, or it can be a slow build. Distress is troubling because no one falls down a mountain without a few marks. Perhaps you have bought a piece of furniture or fabric that has been "distressed." These pieces are known for their marks and scars. Without addressing the results of distress in our lives for healing, our bodies and minds remain raw and open wide to more distress, wider and deeper marks and scars.[35]

35　Stephen W. Porges, "The Polyvagal Theory: New Insights into Adaptive Reactions of the Autonomic Nervous

Distress pushes us over the edge, sending us tumbling from the crest of a mountain.

Our mental health takes a hit when we're distressed. Left untended, distress can cause us to become more anxious, run a higher risk of depression, and have a harder time regulating our emotions.[36] When we live with distress as a constant reality, such as experiencing some form of abuse or when our basic needs are not met, our interpersonal skills suffer. We struggle to learn, and holding down a job or taking care of our hygiene and living space can be challenging.

Distress impacts our physical health too. Our body responds to stress with various chemicals meant to help us survive and reset. After significantly distressing events, our nervous system can become overly attuned or hyperalert to possible stressors. If we are under chronic conditions that are distressing, our body suffers. We might have more headaches or muscle tension. We might have trouble breathing, and we are at greater risk of heart disease.[37]

● ● ● ● ●

The Bible is honest about the presence and nature of distress in a broken world. In the Bible, people experienced the same wide variety of sadness, anxiety, fear, forgottenness, dread, hurt, heartache, hopelessness, and panic as we do today. The Bible frequently refers to the stressors of life or the distress we experience as "trouble." This trouble can come from inside us, but it can also originate from the actions of others around us or from the world at large. Lamentations 1:20 identifies distress that results from our own rebellion:

System," *Cleveland Clinic Journal of Medicine* 76, no. 4 suppl. 2 (April 2009), https://doi.org/10.3949/ccjm.76.s2.17.

36 "Stress," Centre for Addiction and Mental Health, accessed March 11, 2022, https://www.camh.ca/en/health-info/mental-illness-and-addiction-index/stress; "Warning Signs and Risk Factors for Emotional Distress," Substance Abuse and Mental Health Services Administration, last modified November 9, 2021, https://www.samhsa.gov/find-help/disaster-distress-helpline/warning-signs-risk-factors.

37 "Stress Effects on the Body," American Psychological Association, accessed October 11, 2021, https://www.apa.org/topics/stress/body.

Look, O LORD, for I am in distress; my stomach churns; my heart is wrung within me, because I have been very rebellious. In the street the sword bereaves; the house it is like death.

David and his companions experienced distress at the hand of others in 1 Samuel 22:1–2:

David departed from there and escaped to the cave of Adullam. And when his brothers and all his father's house heard it, they went down there to him. And everyone who was in distress, and everyone who was in debt, and everyone who was bitter in soul, gathered to him. And he became commander over them. And there were with him about four hundred men.

Jesus teaches about and ministers to the distress and trouble we all encounter in this world in John 16:33 (NIV):

I have told you these things, so that in Me you may have peace. In this world you will have trouble. But take heart! I have overcome the world.

When we hear God or Jesus say things like "Take heart!" or "Fear not!" we tend to hear them as commandments or judgments. It's helpful to be aware of where we might be reading an emotional position into Jesus' words where there is none, or at least not one we are privy to. The Bible is meant to be read in context—not only the context of the words of a passage but also the context of the person and work of Jesus Christ, which informs us about who God is and who is speaking when we read His Word. Once something is taken out of that original context, we can lose sight of the values that help interpret it.

"Take heart!" and "Fear not!" describe the grace and promises available to us in Christ, rather than tell us who we should be emotionally. John 3:16–17 reminds us of Jesus' purpose, which is never disconnected from His emotional state:

> For God so loved the world, that He gave His only Son, that whoever believes in Him should not perish but have eternal life. For God did not send His Son into the world to condemn the world, but in order that the world might be saved through Him.

Jesus Himself experienced distress. Two specific instances include the death of Jesus' friend Lazarus and the prayerful night in the Garden of Gethsemane before His arrest. The Gethsemane account displays Jesus' distress particularly well: "He took with Him Peter and James and John, and began to be greatly **distressed** and **troubled**. And He said to them, 'My soul is very sorrowful, even to death. Remain here and watch'" (Mark 14:33–34, emphasis added). God seems to know we need it written clearly across the page so that we may believe Jesus is our great High Priest who sympathizes or empathizes with us in every moment (Hebrews 4:15).

Being connected to Jesus in our distress is no small thing, because distress feels inherently disconnecting. Distress sparks our internal drive to check out, a physiological process called disassociating. We might check out in small ways (mental grocery lists and scrolling mindlessly through our phone) or in bigger ways (shutting down or feeling mentally disconnected from our body). Distress might come from scary things, but the experience itself can feel scary as well. These two things—a stressful situation and our experience of that distress—can compound and engulf us in what seems like ever-growing distress.

Jesus has been there. Luke 22:42–44 calls this experience "agony":

> [Jesus said,] "Father, if You are willing, remove this cup from Me. Nevertheless, not My will, but Yours, be

done." And there appeared to Him an angel from heaven, strengthening Him. And being in agony He prayed more earnestly; and His sweat became like great drops of blood falling down to the ground.

All of us generally want a life with zero distress. Jesus said it out loud, so we can admit that distress is hard for us as well. We live in a broken world that's full of beauty, sure, but also full of soul-wrenching, mind-stretching, pore-draining struggle. The word *distress* allows us to be honest about those struggles, to bring them to the Father, to plead, to beat our breasts, to ask questions, and to ask for more from God—more of His presence, more of His help.

●　●　●　●　●

Distress is inevitable; we will all experience it at some point. But we are not left alone in our distress. God gives us people and resources to help us deal with our distress through care and connection. Jesus died for our salvation and gives us tools for our daily life. God is oriented toward restoration; all things will be restored one day when He comes back for us, but He also brings that restoration into our days now. God's restoration resources might look like therapy, medicine, books, a good Bible study, or conversation with friends. One form of therapy, dialectical behavior therapy (DBT), teaches skills for distress tolerance, including validation, awareness, and coping skills. Sometimes—oftentimes—we could use a little help figuring out what's distressing us, why it's distressing, and what God has knit into our body to help us heal when we are in distress.

> ### God gives us people and resources to help us deal with our distress through care and connection.

God gives us His restoration and care in many forms. Even when it feels far from true, God is for us, not against us. Isaiah 43:2–4 speaks to the heart of distress tolerance:

> When you pass through the waters, I will be with you; and through the rivers, they shall not overwhelm you; when you walk through fire you shall not be burned, and the flame shall not consume you. For I am the LORD your God, the Holy One of Israel, your Savior. I give Egypt as your ransom, Cush and Seba in exchange for you. Because you are precious in My eyes, and honored, and I love you, I give men in return for you, peoples in exchange for your life.

Jesus, in His own distress, exchanged His life for yours and mine. We can stand on this foundation when we are stretched to our limits. We may be distressed. We may reach our limit when the brokenness of life reveals itself. We may feel like our souls are drained and hearts shattered. We may stomp our feet and need to yell for help. But redemption is not only a long-ago moment. Jesus' redemption for us is alive here and now. While we'd rather do away with it, distress can actually highlight Christ's active redemption and restoration in our lives, bringing out His care in bold and beautiful ways. Do we want to relive those moments? No. Oh please, no. Do we always understand them? No. Is there a clear "greater purpose" to our struggles? Not always. Yet, the promise remains: "When you pass through the waters, I will be with you; and through the rivers, they shall not overwhelm you; when you walk through fire you shall not be burned, and the flame shall not consume you" (Isaiah 43:2).

NOTICE AND NAME DISTRESS

- What experiences of distress can you recall in your own life?
- What does distress look and feel like to you?
- Who or what helped you in your moments of distress?

Related words: sorrow, anxiety, troubled, grief, dread, terror, afflicted, mourning, worry, anguish, woe, oppression, overwhelmed, fear, panic, consumed

WEARINESS

My sister Kelly's hugs were a source of strength in my childhood.

When I was very young, it was just my mom and me. Then, one day, life was different. I had a dad and sisters.

Nothing was better than having sisters. A whole new world opened up for me: hair braiding, Sisters Club meetings, arguments over who had to sit in the middle seat of the car. (As the youngest, it was always me.)

Sometimes we don't know what we're missing until change waltzes in, uninvited and presumptuous. Life didn't seem empty before my dad and my sisters. Yet, there was a distinct before and after. Before had grief and my mom's tears, but also the bright light of her smile. After had my dad's hamburgers and Kelly's hugs.

I can feel Kelly's hugs as I talk about them now, her arms wrapped tight around me, her chin resting on my head. Kelly is four years older than me, and it seems she's always been a foot taller. When I had a bad day, when I felt excluded or less than, when I was sad or confused, Kelly's hugs were there. Kelly was a refuge when life seemed uncertain.

Looking back, I understand that seven-year-old Heidi was fun and precocious but also weary. With the loss of my father and the weight of my mother's widowhood afterward, I was tired. I met life's trouble before I could use the bathroom independently. Who wouldn't be weary? Kids carry the weights of life differently, adapting and adjusting, integrating it into themselves, making it work. Kelly's hugs were a place of refuge and rest when I didn't know I needed it. As God brought this simple thing into my life, He also brought His strength tucked way down deep, making the toil and trouble more manageable one day at a time.

●　●　●　●　●

Weariness is an emotion of time. One day's struggle is less likely to create weariness than twenty or two hundred days'. If we listen closely, we can often hear weariness in the voices of the elderly—not because life isn't beautiful, but because their bones carry the years of unsolvable problems, lost relationships, and holding on tightly to God through it all. There is a particular weariness in the faces of parents who lost their child too soon and in the soldier or social worker who has seen too much. Weariness comes from the slow drain of life or life's specific circumstances.

●　●　●　●　●

The Bible characterizes weariness by the physical feeling of it:

> I am weary with my moaning; every night I flood my bed with tears; I drench my couch with my weeping. My eye wastes away because of grief; it grows weak because of all my foes. (Psalm 6:6–7)
> I am weary with my crying out; my throat is parched. My eyes grow dim with waiting for my God. More in number than the hairs of my head are those who hate me without cause; mighty are those who would destroy me, those who attack me with lies. What I did not steal must I now restore? (Psalm 69:3–4)

Weariness is not limited to a long life or deep trauma. Isaiah 40:30–31 confirms the weariness of youth, the exhaustion that can come to even the smallest among us in a broken world:

> Even youths shall faint and be weary, and young men shall fall exhausted; but they who wait for the LORD shall renew their strength; they shall mount up with wings like eagles; they shall run and not be weary; they shall walk and not faint.

Weariness expands out from tiredness and brings a recognition of our vulnerability. In the Book of Judges, an enemy of the people of God, Sisera, is finally put to death in the vulnerability of his weariness. Battle and running and plotting has worn him out, and his guard is down.

Jeremiah, a prophet in the seventh century before Christ, expresses before God the weariness of speaking out and speaking up among people with hearts closed to hearing:

> For whenever I speak, I cry out, I shout, "Violence and destruction!" For the word of the LORD has become for me a reproach and derision all day long. If I say, "I will not mention Him, or speak any more in His name," there is in my heart as it were a burning fire shut up in my bones, and **I am weary with holding it in**, and I cannot. (Jeremiah 20:8–9, emphasis added)

We become wearied living in a broken world and trusting and following God in that world. It is wearisome to seek justice, to find justice at times, and yet need to ask for it again and again in the face of oppression. Weariness comes as we climb the hill of cancer or loss or poverty and find more hills as we crest each one. The Book of Ecclesiastes speaks to the connection between weariness and boredom—the monotony of brokenness with no solutions and often more questions.

We become wearied living in a broken world and trusting and following God in that world.

God meets our weariness with validation and understanding. God gets weary too. Isaiah 1:14 tells us He gets weary of Israel's lip service and sacrifices without heart. I wonder if He ever gets weary of humanity's propensity toward injustice, our inability to listen or be nice to one another. God longs for more for His creation.

John 4 (verse 6 in particular) shows us the weariness of Jesus Himself. He is weary from travel and possibly from people's relentless opinions and unending speculation about His character and intentions. Jesus is weary because He is human. As a man, He clothed Himself in our human vulnerability rather than shielding Himself from it. He took on the cloak of human needs like safety, refuge, and sleep. Jesus found safety and refuge in the One He could trust the most: the Father. He entrusted His weariness to the One who is strength. He relied on the Holy Spirit when His earthly body and mind had nothing left. Like me with my sister's hugs, He folded Himself into the invisible arms of the One who loved Him most.

● ● ● ● ●

When our capacity runs out, our own weariness is best met with God's refuge, as well as the flame of connection. My sister's hugs spoke volumes with no words. They said, "You matter here. You are not alone." She honored my capacity for weariness and even expanded it at times. Through the refuge of her affection, I could keep going. I absorbed hope through her presence. God offers hope in His presence through His Word and His Spirit, telling us, "I will never leave you. You are beloved."

Moses experienced his share of weariness and often doubted his capacity—he even argued his capability with God Himself! But time and time again God showed Moses that He would graciously equip him for and sustain him in the work. Moses also found connection and support in his siblings (at times . . . you know how siblings are) and through co-leaders who walked with him in the exodus and beyond. Still, it must have been wearisome to wander the desert, to lose the elderly and birth new babies and continue circling the promise. During one wilderness battle, the secret weapon was for Moses to hold up his arms. If his arms dropped, the people of God started losing; while his arms held steady, they won. Why this system was God pleasing, I have no idea. Sometimes we don't know. But through this system, the people of God got an important reminder:

> But Moses' hands grew weary, so they took a stone and put it under him, and he sat on it, while Aaron and Hur held up his hands, one on one side, and the other on the other side. So his hands were steady until the going down of the sun. (Exodus 17:12)

We are most capable when we rely on God and our connection with God and one another. I'm guessing Moses still needed an ice bath after they won the battle. The capability and connection don't solve the weariness, but they do help us walk through the weariness and into God's mercies. God may bring us to a new season eventually, one where our feet have a little more pep and a lighter step. But if all we get is the ability to call weariness by name through the journey, we have gained capacity, and we often open our eyes to the connections all around us. Because what we do have in our weariness is people. As tempting as it is to disconnect from those who love us, we need their energy in our weariness. We need their laughter and smiles and hugs. We need a refuge from weariness, where God gives more grace.

We are most capable when we rely on God and our connection with God and one another.

Psalm 90 speaks to the importance of connection in weariness. Moses wrote it as a prayer over his weariness and also the short breadth of life. The whole psalm uses plural words—*we* and *our* and *us*. When weariness walks in, it's helpful to remember that we are not alone.

The psalm is not cheerful, but it is honest. Life is honest. My dad died. My mom was sad. I wish it were different, but instead I have to navigate what is real. Moses had to navigate what was real. Refuge is the answer to weariness. That refuge comes in God's steadfast love and in His gift of things like a sister's hugs. We never have to navigate alone. Always, we are "us."

> Satisfy us in the morning with Your steadfast love, that we may rejoice and be glad all our days. Make us glad for as many days as You have afflicted us, and for as many years as we have seen evil. Let Your work be shown to Your servants, and Your glorious power to their children. Let the favor of the Lord our God be upon us, and establish the work of our hands upon us; yes, establish the work of our hands! (Psalm 90:14–17)

NOTICE AND NAME WEARINESS

- What stuff of life leaves you feeling weary?
- What does weariness look and feel like for you?
- Who or what helps you feel capable and connected in your weariness?

Related words: toil, dull, hopeless, weighed down, lose heart, tired, sad, boredom, longing, vulnerable, helpless, refuge, comfort, provision, protection, agency, help, safety

INDIGNATION

In all my education, I rode the school bus for a short 165 days or so during sixth grade. That adventure ended abruptly when a boy on the bus made sexual advances toward several of us girls and, upon finding no interest, started using derogatory terms that I won't repeat. I'm not sure I entirely understood the terms, but I knew they were insulting. I was indignant.

In the shock of the moment, it never dawned on me to go to a trustworthy adult for help. There was rarely a time when I felt unsupported by the adults around me, but the nature of the problem was embarrassing to say the least. Sixth-grade girls were not taught how to deal with sexual propositions and disparagement in the early 1990s, nor were our parents envisioning we would be dealing with it at such a young age. After one particularly demeaning slur aimed in my direction, I stood up to all four feet nine inches of myself and slapped the offender across the face. The next day, I was called to the principal's office and kicked off the bus.

My mom and dad showed up to the same principal's office in a flash, full of their own indignation. After they met with the principal, I never rode the bus again, but neither did the boy in question. I'm still grateful to my parents for teaching me a lesson they didn't know I needed: indignation has a purpose, and justice is a group effort.

● ● ● ● ●

Indignation is a complex emotion on the same spectrum as anger, annoyance, and frustration. What sets indignation apart, however, is the companion of grief, rather than anger alone. In the anger and grief of indignation, we want different or better, bringing forward a desire for justice that lights a fire inside us. The English word comes from Latin, combining the prefix *in-*, meaning "not," and the root *dignus*, meaning "worth."[38] Indignation is an emotional response triggered by seeing someone robbed of their sense of dignity or worth or experiencing it ourselves.

When the apostle Paul wrote a letter to the Church in Corinth, he was concerned about people taking advantage of the weaknesses of others and how that could rob them of their dignity. In Paul's day, that often happened when people tried to add requirements to the Gospel or propagated false gospels. Paul wrote of the anxiety and indignation that comes from being a leader and seeing others harmed by such falsehoods: "And, apart from other things, there is the daily pressure on me of my anxiety for all the churches. Who is weak, and I am not weak? Who is made to fall, and I am not indignant?" (2 Corinthians 11:28–29).

When someone leads another person into sin, they also hand over shame. Lives and relationships that lack truth often lack boundaries as well. While having no boundaries might seem like freedom, it's not safe for anyone, which is the opposite of freedom. Such relationships have consequences: victims whose dignity is swept away, left wondering about their worth. Paul wanted God's grace for people through truth. God is both love and justice commingled, not one without the other.

---

38 Online Etymology Dictionary, s.v. "Indignation (n.)," accessed September 17, 2021, https://www.etymonline .com/word/indignation.

●　　●　　●　　●　　●

Sometimes people steal others' God-given sense of worth by leaving them as outsiders. Jesus expresses indignation when the disciples criticized parents and other adults for bringing children to see Him:

> And they were bringing children to Him that He might touch them, and the disciples rebuked them. But when Jesus saw it, He was indignant and said to them, "Let the children come to Me; do not hinder them, for to such belongs the kingdom of God. Truly, I say to you, whoever does not receive the kingdom of God like a child shall not enter it." And He took them in His arms and blessed them, laying His hands on them. (Mark 10:13–16)

The idea that children would be robbed of relationship and healing incensed Jesus, lit Him on fire. Jesus was moved to action. We can hear His grief in the anger of His rebuke. Imagine a world where God does not want children or any other segment of the population. Jesus immediately spoke with the disciples so the ministry could reflect God's inclusion of all people in the saving message of the Gospel.

The grief aspects of indignation are clearest perhaps in John 11, with the account of the death and resurrection of Jesus' friend Lazarus. Jesus sees Lazarus's sister Mary weeping. He sees people all around Him weeping. He responds emotionally:

> Now when Mary came to where Jesus was and saw Him, she fell at His feet, saying to Him, "Lord, if You had been here, my brother would not have died." When Jesus saw her weeping, and the Jews who had come with her also weeping, He was deeply moved in His spirit and greatly troubled. (John 11:32–33)

One author clarifies what can be lost from the Greek text in the English translation, noting that the Greek root of the words describing Jesus as "deeply moved" provides imagery of a snort, harrumph, or other vocalization.[39] In this instance, the indignance of Christ doesn't have a specific target. Is He grieved by the brokenness of the world? Is He impacted by the tears He knows could have been avoided had humankind not sought a life outside of God's boundaries? Does Jesus share in the frustration over the seemingly nonsensical loss of a life gone too soon?

Sighs and harrumphs, snorts and groans are good for the soul at times. I see these things naturally more often in the therapy room because it's a safe place to let out the physical burden of indignation. If we let that emotion out in safe places, it's less likely to jump up on us and leave us standing shocked on a school bus with one red hand and no good way to explain ourselves.

Eight chapters after the account of Jesus' indignation at death in John 11, death would rob Jesus of His own dignity. Jesus knows that death robs every human of dignity in their time. Death brings with it naked exposure. We are all powerless in our mortality. Death reveals our need, our body's tendency toward disintegration with nothing to stop it. Death also points us to our desperation for Jesus Christ's salvation. Death should make us angry and hurt and leave us wanting something better. The idea that Jesus is indignant at death itself fits well with Jesus' actions of restoration we see next in John 11. Lazarus is resurrected, returned fully to life. His family received an inexplicable gift. This great gift was a precursor to God's greater gift of restoration offered to humankind. Throughout Scripture, we find a God who, amidst the chaos humans continuously create, has an emotional response, mourns, and also rescues us from the indignity

---

39 F. Scott Spencer, *Passions of the Christ: The Emotional Life of Jesus in the Gospels* (Grand Rapids, MI: Baker Academic, 2021), 57–59; Strong's Concordance, s.v. "1690. embrimaomai," https://biblehub.com /greek/1690.htm.

sin and death bring into our lives—sometimes in the here and now, sometimes longer term.

● ● ● ● ●

Indignation is an eyes-wide-open emotion. The language of indignation can encourage us because it offers movement to the grief and anger we feel when we look at a world full of injustice, whether that's explicit sexual aggression thrown at girls, a life taken at the hand of another, racial injustice, hurtful words without forethought, or however injustice appears in our lives. It's not hard to find something. The movement of indignation reminds us God is active, working in the places where we'd like to see justice.

In this desire for movement, our indignation propels us forward. Forward doesn't always mean reacting instantly. We can dig deeper to find out the full story. We can ask questions. We might seek wisdom and help from others to sort through the convoluted things of our lives and this world.

We also do well to remember that, unlike Jesus' indignance, our indignance is not perfect. Our perception may be flawed. Sometimes we detect injustice and feel indignance where there is only inconvenience or disruption. Worse, we might perceive a need for indignance when we see dignity being restored to those robbed of it in the first place. Through our sin and belief in our own righteousness, we can easily cause further injustice because of misplaced indignation. But our indignance will serve us best when we check it against God's justice and His grace.

Our indignance will serve us best when we check it against God's justice and His grace.

God's justice sometimes includes His hate and wrath—often the most uncomfortable emotions for us to understand in the Bible. Yet, these are linked to His justice and desire that dignity be upheld in humans. We impact God. What we do impacts God. He desires better for us, as He describes in Isaiah 1:16–17:

> Wash yourselves; make yourselves clean; remove the evil
> of your deeds from before My eyes; cease to do evil, learn
> to do good; seek justice, correct oppression; bring justice
> to the fatherless, plead the widow's cause.

God's desire is for us and for all people. Our righteousness comes from Christ alone, not from our opinions, ideas, or indignance. When indignation rises to the surface, whether on the school bus, while watching the evening news, or when interacting with a neighbor, may God guide our questions, our hearts, and our conversation so that His justice reigns and not our own.

NOTICE AND NAME INDIGNANCE

- When have you experienced indignance?
- What issues of justice do you see around you today?
- How have you seen God restore dignity for a person or people group?

Related words: annoyed, angry, frustrated, irritated, bitter, unfair, justice, injustice, incensed, grieve, displeased

CONTEMPT

Try as she might, our daughter couldn't figure out how to roll her eyes.

When my oldest daughter, Macee, was a sophomore in high school, she was in her first one-act play. A prominent feature of her character was irritability, annoyance, and sarcasm. At one point in rehearsals, Macee came home with her own annoyance: she couldn't roll her eyes. At fifteen years old, she could conjure up an impeccable British accent and tears on cue, but she couldn't lift her eyes to the ceiling to show contempt?

I'll take the blame. Or maybe I blame the Holy Spirit. Long before I studied the research on contempt and eye rolling, I knew the two were linked. Our house has very few rules, but "no eye rolling" is one of them. In our house, you can argue, you can pester, and you can tease. You can even be sarcastic if it's understood by both people and done in love. But flagrant displays of contempt—eye rolling, mocking, dismissive tones, name calling? Off limits.

Macee did learn to roll her eyes for the play. We watched her, glowing with pride, ironically, mostly because we knew it took effort. When contempt takes effort, all is right with the world, if only for a moment.

● ● ● ● ●

Our world hands out contempt in so many forms, some more or less obvious than eye rolling. Contempt is a form of pride that is fueled by underlying negative thoughts about someone.[40] The Gottman Institute, a leader in research around relationship dynamics, has researched the emotion of contempt for years. This research reveals that contempt is one of the most destructive forces in any relationship, but particularly intimate ones. In fact, their research across thousands of diverse couples shows contempt as the single greatest predictor of divorce.[41]

When we are feeling contemptuous, we elevate ourselves above the person in front of us. Common phrases related to contempt, whether spoken or left as thoughts, include "I would never . . ." and "If only they did it my way . . ." Contempt is one expression of the way our emotions link to our perceptions. We feel contempt when we perceive someone as wrong or perceive their thoughts, ideas, or opinions as less worthy than our own. It is an emotion of disconnection, or turning against the person in front of us rather than turning toward them to attempt understanding.

Emotions are not disconnected. They are connected to our thoughts and actions. Therapists and other mental health professionals use a simple graphic called the CBT triangle to help people understand these connections. Each segment of the triangle has a different word: *thoughts*, *feelings*, and *behaviors*. For any of our actions in a certain situation, we can fill in the different thoughts and feelings that were present alongside the action. Connecting these dots helps us see the fuller picture.

Emotions are not disconnected. They are connected to our thoughts and actions.

Cognitive behavioral therapy (CBT) centers on the theory that thoughts, emotions, and actions are all linked, feeding one another. Contempt starts somewhere on that CBT triangle, but it's not always

---

40   Ellie Lisitsa, "The Four Horsemen: Contempt," The Gottman Institute, accessed March 7, 2022, https://www .gottman.com/blog/the-four-horsemen-contempt/.

41   Lisitsa, "The Four Horsemen: Contempt."

in the same place. Some emotions seem to come and go with a swift breeze or appear out of nowhere, but the emotion of contempt is not likely to come out of left field. Contempt grows from a seed that is watered and nurtured. We feed the contempt inside of us toward someone because it feels good. It feels validating to believe that we are better than they are, especially when we feel like we are not being heard or we want to protect the "rightness" of our ideas or beliefs. In this way, contempt becomes stronger and stronger, fueled by negative thoughts and perceptions, more easily activated over time.

●　●　●　●　●

The Bible also reveals the destructiveness of contempt. There are no instances of God throwing out contempt on humankind, even in His anger and wrath. The Bible talks about God's hate in some circumstances—for example, His hate of humanity's ability to destroy—and God's regret when humans showed themselves violent and unrepentant before the flood in Noah's day. But we never find God declaring worthlessness over His creation and especially not over us as created human beings. God is more complex than that, and so are His emotions.

When we read of God's hate or experience our own penchant for contempt, it's important to allow for tension within our emotions. God is both perfect Law and perfect Gospel. He holds His own emotional tensions of love and hate perfectly. We are messy. Some emotions, like contempt, serve as mirrors of the Law in our lives. We take an aspect of God's good gifts, like justice, too far into contempt. Taking things too far is very human. We need the Gospel to meet us in our contempt. God's gift of Jesus, the sacrifice of His Son, reveals a God who is not contemptuous toward us, even in the most challenging aspects of our humanity.

One of the most powerful ways we can minimize the emotion of contempt in our hearts and minds is by acknowledging our *capacity* for contempt. By allowing the tension of Law and Gospel in our emotional lives, we understand ourselves more. Contempt is clearly an emotion that reveals the "old Adam" within us. Our old Adam—so intricately linked to sin, original and our own—will be a part of us until Christ comes again. But in holding together both Law and Gospel, letting the emotion be more complicated and less one-sided, contempt can also be a "new Adam" emotion. Emotions like contempt make clear the work of Jesus Christ as He daily drowns and raises our whole selves in His death and resurrection. Christ came for the old Adam so that we don't have to hold on to the shame or contempt.

● ● ● ● ●

Scripture provides two crystal-clear examples of contempt. The first details the destructive power of contempt in a marriage or household. In the second, an authority figure uses contempt to demean someone in order to elevate his own power. Contempt doesn't have to be as loud or obvious as it is in these stories, but I think we can find plenty of instances around us like these today.

Our first example appears in 2 Samuel 6, when King David and his troops brought home the ark of the covenant. Before the resurrection of Christ, the ark served as the very presence of the Lord among God's people, and this precious ark had been stolen by Israel's enemies. In time, David saw to it that the presence of God was once again at home with His people.

In celebration of the ark's return to the city of Jerusalem, David danced before the Lord in little more than his Underoos. He danced as an offering, a gift of joy, gratitude, and vulnerability before God. However, his wife, Michal, did not see the gift. She greeted David with hostile sarcasm, criticism, and contempt:

> And David returned to bless his household. But Michal the daughter of Saul came out to meet David and said, "How the king of Israel honored himself today, uncovering himself today before the eyes of his servants' female servants, as one of the vulgar fellows shamelessly uncovers himself!" And David said to Michal, "It was before the LORD, who chose me above your father and above all his house, to appoint me as prince over Israel, the people of the LORD—and I will celebrate before the LORD. I will make myself yet more contemptible than this, and I will be abased in your eyes. But by the female servants of whom you have spoken, by them I shall be held in honor." (2 Samuel 6:20–22)

The Hebrew terms for *contempt* and *honor* here are held in tension, with *contempt* being a littleness and *honor* being a largeness. God's kingdom is one of equality. While we all have various roles in our households or workplaces, no one is larger or smaller than another in God's eyes, and we're called to treat one another as such.

The second example is in the Book of Acts. As the apostles and Early Church leaders worked to spread the Gospel, they encountered persecution in many forms. In one instance, the contempt of both the Roman authorities and the high priest Ananias is clear in their physical assaults. Paul's response to Ananias is notable. In the passage below, notice how Paul brings respect back into the room:

> And looking intently at the council, Paul said, "Brothers, I have lived my life before God in all good conscience up to this day." And the high priest Ananias commanded those who stood by him to strike him on the mouth. Then Paul said to him, "God is going to strike you, you whitewashed wall! Are you sitting to judge me according to the law,

and yet contrary to the law you order me to be struck?" Those who stood by said, "Would you revile God's high priest?" And Paul said, "I did not know, brothers, that he was the high priest, for it is written, 'You shall not speak evil of a ruler of your people.'" (Acts 23:1–5)

● ● ● ● ●

One psalmist recognizes the recurrence, maybe even routineness, of contempt in the world around us:

To You I lift up my eyes, O You who are enthroned in the heavens! Behold, as the eyes of servants look to the hand of their master, as the eyes of a maidservant to the hand of her mistress, so our eyes look to the LORD our God, till He has mercy upon us. Have mercy upon us, O LORD, have mercy upon us, for we have had more than enough of contempt. Our soul has had more than enough of the scorn of those who are at ease, of the contempt of the proud. (Psalm 123)

Our world has plenty of places for shame to live. Shame exists because sin exists. The sin in us and around us will bring shame into our hearts and minds. But contempt is different from the shame we all battle as a result of brokenness. Contempt involves the *act* of shaming, throwing shame at another person. Contempt comes out of our faulty human judgments. The Gottman Institute notes in their research that showing respect and appreciation brings healing, repairing the rupture that contempt introduces to a relationship.[42] This research complements our Christian understanding of daily dying and rising as baptized children of God. The Holy Spirit is our help, our coun-

---

42 Ellie Lisitsa, "The Four Horsemen: The Antidotes," The Gottman Institute, accessed March 11, 2022, https://www.gottman.com/blog/the-four-horsemen-the-antidotes/.

selor, and our guide in our moments of contempt; He helps us to find respect, fondness, admiration, and appreciation again.

Contempt comes out of our faulty human judgments.

We all have likely thrown contempt out at other people. Whether it's tossed out in our family relationships because we have heard the same story or complaint a thousand times or directed at the TSA agent slowing down our travel by trying to do their job, contempt makes the existence of original sin in us painfully obvious. Again, sin and hurtfulness are at times our human nature, not always our conscious action. Putting the word *contempt* back into our vocabulary is an important step in recognizing our capacity for emotions gone awry, keeping them in their place as informants rather than leaders, and living in the grace of the Gospel of Jesus Christ. Jesus makes it possible to stitch repair into any situation.

We won't be perfect, but with honesty we are more likely to squelch the sparks of contempt that appear in us or around us. Shame is not combated with more shame; judgment is not combated with more judgment. Instead, we face contempt with the Pauline response: respect toward others and respect for ourselves. We see through God's lens. We lay our hurtful and judgmental natures before God and ask for forgiveness. We look at ourselves and one another as He looks at us through Jesus Christ.

When the world gives contempt again and again, when contempt rises inside of us, we lift our eyes to the throne and see mercy.

NOTICE AND NAME CONTEMPT

- Around what people or kinds of people are you most likely to experience the rise of contempt?
- What does contempt look and feel like for you?
- What might be some helpful reminders for you of God's value for all human life?

Related words: disregard, derision, revile, impudence, hard-hearted, stiff-necked, resistant, hurtful, disdain, look down upon, disconnection, shame, scorn, denigration, judgment

PERPLEXITY

I'm not sure if our dog Cottonball was a boy or a girl. Cottonball was mangy and gentle and came with our house when we bought it. She roamed our acreage with a free spirit, showing up only when she sensed we had a bad day and needed love or when leftovers were thrown over the side of the deck.

But then she seemed to vanish into thin air. After several days, I asked my dad if he had seen Cottonball. He hemmed and hawed in the way parents do when they are not sure whether information is too grown up for the child asking. I know my dad would have protected my heart forever, but hearts grow up alongside bodies. In the end, my dad described Cottonball as "gone."

Cottonball's absence and the word *gone* to describe what I eventually found out was her death was the first moment I had the distinct feeling of being perplexed by life, loss, and adult problems.

I didn't understand "gone." What is death when you are a kid? It's a word too meaty to manage quite yet. But I was doubtful and confused. I was anxious for Cottonball, out there away from our house and pond and woods. I was sad, longing for her soft fur and its mess of burrs.

● ● ● ● ●

Childhood is full perplexity—a mix of cognitive confusion and a distinct emotional component of uncertainty. The doubt, anxiety, sadness, and longing I experienced are related to perplexity, sharing an emotional orbit.

Sometimes life happens without the order and routine we have grown to expect from it. Order is stabilizing. The disorder of brokenness and its consequences brings waves of reality into our lives—some of which we can understand, some that take time, and others that have no explanation among humans. The sudden awareness of disorder feels destabilizing. Welcome to the world of perplexity.

As we grow older, perplexity occasionally carries feelings of inadequacy as well. Most of the experiences that leave us perplexed are normal experiences of confronting a beautiful and broken life, but they twist around inside of us, pushing mental buttons and forming thoughts of inadequacy:

"It isn't supposed to be this way."

"I should be able to understand this."

"I thought I had my ducks in a row."

"What's wrong with me that this is hard? What's wrong with me that this is happening to me?"

When a high school classmate of mine was killed in a car accident, I remember the funeral was heavy with loss but also weighted with a desire for answers: Why did this happen to someone so young? Where was God's protection when one of us needed it? Teens especially need support in these moments because our culture transmits that teenagers are old enough for bigger things. No one says out loud that death will always make us feel small again, no matter our age and wisdom. No one says out loud that it's not our job to have life's answers, whether we're nine years old, nineteen, or ninety.

Perplexity is more complex than confusion. Confusion is the feeling that things are mixed up in our minds and need some sorting. Perplexity occurs when we feel confusion along with the sense that there is an answer we can't seem to reach or find. It can come with a sense of shame because we feel like we should know the answer.

However, the feeling of perplexity can also come with a sense of awe and wonder. When we feel perplexed but connect what is unknown to God and the awareness that God knows the answer, we experience stability once again. By linking our confusion and longing to know with the truth of God, we can feel connected through our sense of perplexity instead of disconnected. Sometimes in our perplexity we need to be reminded of God's might and His mystery, His enormity, and His ability to keep all things in His care.

Sometimes in our perplexity we need to be reminded of God's might and His mystery.

Our brains can't always manage to make that connection on our own though. We will likely experience times when we need someone else to help us. When someone reaches out to help us connect some dots, we are more likely to see awe and wonder in our perplexity rather than feel only foggy or lost. We handle the emotional experience of perplexity better in relationship, where your piece of the understanding puzzle is different from mine and the pieces were made to fit together. It's the feeling that comes when, as adults, you and your sisters discuss the loss of your childhood dog and welcome both the laughter and the tears surrounding whatever "gone" meant, and your memories together bring some levity to what was only heavy before.

● ● ● ● ●

Experiences of perplexity in the Bible tend to be encouraging because they reveal that it's a universal experience. Those of us in the twenty-first century aren't the only people perplexed by the disorder and concerns of this world. Every person throughout time and place has likely found life perplexing. Even more encouraging in our spiritual walk, maybe, is the revelation that God was as perplexing to the people of Babylon, Rome, and Israel as God is to the people in America, Myanmar, and Malawi today.

The Bible also makes clear that perplexity isn't about how smart we are. In the Book of Daniel, the smartest men in the kingdom were perplexed by the pallor and impending death of the healthy King Belshazzar (5:9). We are all simple humans before God, then and now. Humans aren't the only ones who find themselves perplexed either! In Joel 1:18, the cattle were perplexed by the trauma and devastation the locusts left behind when God usually sheltered them from such things. If cattle are allowed to be perplexed, so are we.

The Hebrew terms for *perplexed* are related to wandering or entanglement.[43] They remind us that we *are* wandering in this life to some degree. We are pilgrims with a destination in mind, but sometimes the journey is confusing. When we feel tangled up in our understanding by the disorder around us, we can turn to God. His kingdom and restoration are what we were made for, where we are headed. He knows all things when we only know some.

We are pilgrims with a destination in mind, but sometimes the journey is confusing.

The Greek Scriptures more pointedly acknowledge the feelings of being at a loss in perplexity.[44] We see Herod experience perplexity when John the Baptist speaks the truth of the Gospel to him (Mark 6; Luke 9). We also see this perplexity in the disciples at the resurrection of Jesus (Luke 24) and in Peter when the Holy Spirit clarifies God's promises and plans to include the Gentiles in His kingdom (Acts 10).

Perplexity is human. In 2 Corinthians 4:6–9, Paul speaks directly to the unique feeling of perplexity within the Christian walk:

---

43 Strong's Concordance, s.v. "943. buk," https://biblehub.com/hebrew/943.htm; Strong's Concordance, s.v. "7672. shebash," https://biblehub.com/hebrew/7672.htm.

44 James W. Voelz, *Mark 1:1–8:26*, Concordia Commentary (St. Louis, MO: Concordia Publishing House, 2013), 403.

For God, who said, "Let light shine out of darkness," has shone in our hearts to give the light of the knowledge of the glory of God in the face of Jesus Christ. But we have this treasure in jars of clay, to show that the surpassing power belongs to God and not to us. We are afflicted in every way, but not crushed; perplexed, but not driven to despair; persecuted, but not forsaken; struck down, but not destroyed.

Again, this is where relationships make a huge difference in lifting the shame that can come from not knowing the answers or being confused. Our attachment to God, or relationship with God, reminds us that being perplexed doesn't take us under.

● ● ● ● ●

Reclaiming the language of perplexity goes a long way in our culture. No one wants to admit when they don't know something. With the information of the internet at our fingertips, we feel like we are *supposed* to know everything. We often judge ourselves and others harshly for not knowing. Imagine the benefit for our emotional health and well-being if we said aloud, "I don't know," or, "It's not my job to know everything, but I know whose job it is."

Knowledge is valuable, but it doesn't determine our worth. We are Christ's, and He connects us to our Father and Enlightener. When we recognize and admit our moments and feelings of perplexity, when we invite others into that connection, we might just get a glimpse of the kind of perplexity we find on the Day of Pentecost:

And they were all filled with the Holy Spirit and began to speak in other tongues as the Spirit gave them utterance. Now there were dwelling in Jerusalem Jews, devout men from every nation under heaven. And at this sound the multitude came together, and they were bewildered, because each one was hearing them speak in his own language. And they were amazed and astonished, saying, "Are not all these who are speaking Galileans? And how is it that we hear, each of us in his own native language? ... We hear them telling in our own tongues the mighty works of God." And all were amazed and perplexed, saying to one another, "What does this mean?" (Acts 2:4–8, 11–12)

Recognizing perplexity is to say unabashedly, "It's complicated." Life and language and explanations are complicated. My dad had no idea how to help me understand the loss of our sweet and mangy ball of fluff. I wish he would have had the language of perplexity. I think it would have allowed him the freedom to say out loud that life is complicated, while still leaving adult problems to the adults. It may have allowed him the freedom to say, "I don't know," and engage in the work of figuring it out together. When we learn to connect with God and others in our sense of perplexity, we get "whoa" and "wow" when we would otherwise have only confusion, inadequacy, and sometimes sorrow. Complicated isn't all bad. Complicated in Christ means restoration and renewal and something more to come.

NOTICE AND NAME PERPLEXITY

- What moments in childhood did you struggle to understand at the time, or maybe still struggle to understand now?

- What does perplexed look and feel like to you?

- Where do you see God's order in this world? Where do you see the disorder of brokenness?

Related words: astonished, confused, puzzled, baffled, complicated, intricate, woven/entangled, doubtful, embarrassed, desiring of order, restless, awe

FELT COMPASSION

Last summer, we moved across the country. Moving means packing and saying a million goodbyes, the exhaustion of finding the grocery store and the DMV, and trying to believe you are capable of building a new life.

In the midst of all the sadness and inconvenience of moving, we found out that one of our kids needed several vaccinations to start school. Finding the grocery store is one thing; finding a family doctor is another. We opted for our friendly local Walgreens, where we learned our health insurance didn't start for a couple more weeks. We told the apologetic pharmacist that we'd just pay for the shots so our son could start school and life.

My husband, teen son, and I stood in line, filling out the forms and chatting about moving, logistics, and life, while our youngest looked through the overpriced selection of Legos nearby. About the time our spot in the line made it up to the multivitamin section, a stranger walked past us and laid what can only be called a small wad of money on the clipboard in my hands.

Her words were fast, and she was gone in a flash: "Moving is hard. Medicine costs money. Welcome to Ludington." My wide eyes met hers for a moment as I stumbled over eloquent phrases like "Um" and "You don't . . ." and "Thank you" before she was past the probiotics and gone. Moving had just gotten a lot easier because of the felt compassion of a stranger in Walgreens.

●　　●　　●　　●　　●

Compassion, according to the internet, is related to want, need, vulnerability, and the wounds the world can leave on us, whether we have been on the planet three days or thirty thousand. The word *compassion* comes from the Latin root words *com*, meaning "with," and *pati*, meaning "to suffer." Who really wants to suffer with someone? Who wants to sit with someone's neediness or become needy beside them? Who wants to become more vulnerable to the pains and trials of this world?

Felt compassion goes even further and deeper than compassion. Felt compassion is a full-body experience—emotional, cognitive, and physical. It is tiring. It touches the soul. It is comfortable with people's questions. Felt compassion also needs boundaries, which means it includes work and consideration.

Particularly in the Bible, felt compassion is an emotional experience different from love, kindness, or comfort; it goes deeper than humility and grace. While it includes all these things, felt compassion adds warmth, acceptance, and *withness*—that particular task of sitting alongside someone in their suffering. For Christians, felt compassion also involves our backstory of forgiveness. The impartial, relentless love given to us in Christ brings to our emotional lives a special hospitality born from gratitude.

Today more than ever, our world could use the language of felt compassion. Compassion brings grace into relationships. Modern American culture often encourages judgment based on people's choices. Being honest that we are all broken, all in need of God's compassion, ignites hope. Felt compassion reaches out no matter the situation; it's not dependent on the circumstances.

● ● ● ● ●

Felt compassion, with its honesty and emotional energy, can sound daunting. The Bible offers four distinct characteristics of felt compassion that make it feel more manageable and help us see where felt compassion is already active in our lives.

First, felt compassion is . . . felt.

In Luke 15:11–32, Jesus tells the story of a family torn apart by choices and complications. In the story, we see a beautiful representation of the felt compassion of God the Father for each of us and those around us. The high point of the story revolves around the compassion of the father for his son:

> [The son said to himself,] "I will arise and go to my father, and I will say to him, 'Father, I have sinned against heaven and before you. I am no longer worthy to be called your son. Treat me as one of your hired servants.'" And he arose and came to his father. But while he was still a long way off, his father saw him and felt compassion, and ran and embraced him and kissed him. (vv. 18–20)

The father not only *has* compassion. He *feels* it. Compassion is an important characteristic of God, but He also allows Himself the emotional experience of compassion—felt compassion. It is a marvel that God engages in this way with humankind. The Greek term used for "compassion" in Luke 15 emphasizes the physicality of the emotion, its felt nature. It's a response from our inner parts to the suffering and hurts of another.[45] It could feel like a gut-wrenching, breath-stealing compassion or just a twinge of compassion. However it presents itself, we feel it in our bodies. The father's felt compassion for his son mirrors God's compassion toward each of us in Jesus. When we feel

---

45 Strong's Concordance, s.v. "4697. splagchnizomai," https://biblehub.com/greek/4697.htm.

compassion, we can allow ourselves to reach out in love as God has reached out to us.

Sometimes, though, when we are confronted with another person's trial, we want to stuff our compassion way down deep. We'd rather ignore the things that are hard and sad, heartbreaking and tiring, uncomfortable and unfixable in life. But as Dr. Brené Brown discovered in her research on shame and emotion,

> We cannot selectively numb emotion. If we numb the dark, we numb the light. If we take the edge off pain and discomfort, we are, by default, taking the edge off joy, love, belonging, and the other emotions that give meaning to our lives.[46]

Life gains meaning when we work through our struggles together, when we allow ourselves to feel compassion and sit with one another in the dark times. Our relationships with one another grow deeper through these connections, and that makes the times of joy and peace even sweeter. Our relationship with God grows too, as we keep learning to share and rely on His grace.

● ● ● ● ●

The second characteristic of felt compassion is impartial grace. The father's compassion was felt while the son was "still a long way off." Felt compassion is not dependent on the recipient's good behavior, healthy perspective, knowledge, or belief system. This characteristic shines brightly in another of Jesus' parables—the story of the Good Samaritan in Luke 10. When the Samaritan man happens upon another man lying in a ditch after being robbed and beaten, he doesn't stop to ask questions about what brought him to this place. Nor did he ask about the other man's religious position, socioeconomic status, or

---

46 Brené Brown, *Dare to Lead: Brave Work. Tough Conversations. Whole Hearts* (New York: Random House Publishing, 2018), 85.

proof of insurance. He felt compassion and he helped. The emotion of felt compassion seems to override our judgments and opinions to let the Holy Spirit work in us in His unique way.

In this way, felt compassion includes dependency. We depend on God for felt compassion. God's heart is to bring salvation to humankind. Because salvation is God's work and not our own, we are free to bring forward compassion rather than judgments and opinions. When we encounter people in need, noticing specific details may help us to bring that compassion forward: What are their mannerisms? What kind of emotions do they seem to be having? We can also ask questions:

"I see that you're crying. Do you want to talk about it?"

"There is a lot happening in your life right now. Can I help in some way?"

"You said the meeting was upsetting. Do you feel angry, sad, unheard? Would you like to say more about your experience?"

Often, though, our actions bring more comfort and love into heavy situations than words do. I didn't have a long conversation with the generous individual who brought compassion to us in Walgreens, and I don't know that I could have explained our tense situation in the moment. But her actions and words didn't bring judgment. Judgment gets in the way of compassion. Felt compassion isn't the time for criticism, no matter how constructive or needed it might seem. Instead, there are times when it's best simply to meet someone's need.

At its core, felt compassion is the impartial grace of Jesus Christ given to us in our own messes and going out in waves to the world around us. We have been forgiven much and therefore we can love much, like the woman in Luke 7. This frees us to lay down our own judgments and pick up God's gifts instead: acceptance in our unearned and undeserved forgiveness and the knowledge of God's overwhelming ability to bring redemption to absolutely anything in this life.

● ● ● ● ●

Loving much doesn't mean compassion has no boundaries though. Instead, we are compassionate about what God has given each of us to notice. God guides us in His gift of felt compassion. We are invited to tune in to the Spirit's nudge (or shout) inside these bodies of ours, to respond to our felt compassion with action. That is the third characteristic of felt compassion: movement. Felt compassion comes up in the moment and seems to want to go!

We see Jesus Himself moved with compassion, as in Matthew 20:30–34 (NASB):

> And two people who were blind, sitting by the road, hearing that Jesus was passing by, cried out, "Lord, have mercy on us, Son of David!" But the crowd sternly warned them to be quiet; yet they cried out all the more, "Lord, Son of David, have mercy on us!" And Jesus stopped and called them, and said, "What do you want Me to do for you?" They said to Him, "Lord, we want our eyes to be opened." Moved with compassion, Jesus touched their eyes; and immediately they regained their sight and followed Him.

Jesus draws on the deep well of His character to bring the emotion of compassion to the surface. Jesus becomes vulnerable to sharing in their suffering and feeling their deep need. It is a radical act, outside the norm of human behavior, to draw on the deep well of who we are and whose we are, in our emotions, rather than only taking what comes up. The movement of felt compassion is also vulnerable because it so often asks for action, and action requires our resources and energy. Felt compassion recognizes that there is always "enough" in Jesus Christ. In all of the passages we've read so far, we see actions—

running, bandaging, paying, acknowledging tears, and ignoring the opinion of the crowd.

● ● ● ● ●

Finally, the fourth characteristic of felt compassion is warmth. Felt compassion connects two or more people, if even for a moment. It's felt both by the person offering compassion and by the person receiving it. Sometimes felt compassion is literally warm. We might feel it in our chest and throat when someone acts compassionately toward us. People also feel the warmth in a room filled with compassion and connection.

The warmth of felt compassion seems connected to biblical hospitality. When felt compassion is present in our homes and faith communities, that warmth communicates a sense of God's presence, reminding everyone involved that He is not a far-off God, but a God who cares and is deeply invested in our lives. In that way, felt compassion can easily lead to Gospel conversations. The woman in Walgreens left me with questions about why she wanted to share what she had with me and who might cause her to do that. Moments like that make us look for God, consciously or subconsciously. The Holy Spirit showing up tends to do that.

Felt compassion can easily lead to Gospel conversations.

● ● ● ● ●

When felt compassion feels far away or hard to hold on to, we can turn to Jesus' compassion in the Gospels. Look for His words and actions of compassion throughout Matthew, Mark, Luke, and John. Contemplate the compassion of His death and resurrection. As we work to reclaim felt compassion in our culture today, I pray you feel the compassion of the Father in your own life. Scripture is alive, and God's compassion is written on every page.

> Praise be to the God and Father of our Lord Jesus Christ, the Father of compassion and the God of all comfort, who comforts us in all our troubles, so that we can comfort those in any trouble with the comfort we ourselves receive from God. For just as we share abundantly in the sufferings of Christ, so also our comfort abounds through Christ. (2 Corinthians 1:3–5 NIV)

NOTICE AND NAME FELT COMPASSION

- What does felt compassion look and feel like for you?
- Which brokenness, injustices, or concerns do you feel compassion toward today?
- Which brokenness, injustices, or concerns are hard for you to feel compassion about?

Related words: grace, mercy, kindness, empathy, sympathy, pity, care, comfort, concern, authenticity, acceptance, belonging, love, moved

CONCLUSION

Decomposing leaves always smell like the start of something to me, like birth instead of death, like finding something rather than losing it. God—in all His love, mercy, wisdom, and complexity—tells the sun when to shine and the leaves when to fall. These cycles are all under His care. And somewhere amid the wetness of spring, when you can smell the death of the leaves nourishing the underwood, God appointed mushroom season.

Most years, my dad took me out into the woods behind our house, paper bag in hand, for a treasure hunt. The morels poked through the dead leaves on the forest floor, life amid the disintegration. Sometimes the treasures were easy to find; other times, harder. I was so excited when we found one that I would run up to the mushroom, shove aside the leaves, and pluck the prize. My dad would remind me in the wizened and judgmental tone of someone who has hunted morels his whole life, "Now, Heidi, you can't just do that. You have to be gentle. There's a technique."

Later, I would come to understand the technique and patience my dad was talking about. Plucking a mushroom with no concern for what lies beneath will likely disrupt the connections of mycelium below the ground. If I pluck one morel willy-nilly, I have a mushroom to eat with dinner, but I also may harm the ecosystem of mycelium— which could result in fewer mushrooms in following years. If instead I clear away a few of the leaves around the mushroom and twist with a gentle hand, I protect the whole system.

• • • • •

The same is true for our emotions: a gentle hand with the things on the surface benefits the health of the whole system.

When we notice an emotion as it comes to the surface of our bodies and lives, we could run up to that emotion, so to speak. We could pluck it, and it would likely be useful for us in some way. Our lives would be better because we didn't ignore that emotion.

But we could also go deeper. We can clear away what surrounds the emotion to better understand it. We can contemplate, articulate, and explore the layers of emotion around that single emotion peeking above the surface. We can intentionally connect with God and find more meaning in our emotions. We can intentionally connect with God's Word and with others around us and find help in our emotions. We can lay our memories of emotional experiences before God and let His grace shine brighter in them to see His redemption in this realm of our lives as well.

• • • • •

I pray you heard no shoulds or musts in this book. They sneak in so easily when we talk about our psyches and our mental health. Instead, I pray you walk away with a broader understanding and a desire to know God deeper—an emotional human creature meeting with an emotional, infinite God.

I pray you heard no shoulds or musts in this book.

I pray you can connect your own experiences to those I have shared from my life. It was a unique joy for me to share so many of my own stories in this book. I wrote them as illustrations but also as a way to honor the emotional work of four-year-old Heidi and twelve-year-old Heidi and all the parts of myself. When we listen to our experiences and stories, we are better able to connect all the messiness and beauty of our lives and emotions to God. We can learn to see Jesus' presence in our most challenging moments when we acknowledge the emotions that feel overwhelming. We learn to see His presence in our brightest moments when we acknowledge and tell of the greatness of our joy. I pray you go from here and collect your own stories, acknowledging your own hard and lovely emotions.

One day, when we see Jesus face-to-face, when tears are no more and the light is so bright we'll be blinded and giddy in God's glory, we will understand these emotions of ours completely. Until then, we can only work each day to understand ourselves and this glorious God of ours through His Word and His gifts, His Son and His sacrifice.

When we experience our emotions as connected to God rather than far from His care and kindness, we will gain insight. We will learn new information and grow in awareness and conviction.

God and His Gospel are connected to all our emotions. God the Father, God the Son, and God the Spirit will continue to be with us, all around this heart, soul, mind, and strength we've been given. May this Gospel change the narrative of what emotions mean, say, and do in our lives today and every day.

LIST OF EMOTIONS IN SCRIPTURE

In my therapy practice, I often use a "feelings wheel" or an emotion word list. When our minds are trying to negotiate emotions, the task of finding language for our emotions can seem intense, so having a list to refer to can help. This list of emotion words in Scripture is not exhaustive, nor is it superior to any other list. It is another tool for connecting our emotions to God and His Gospel.

The terms in this list come from the NIV and ESV translations of the Bible.

For many of the emotion words listed here, the derivative, the expanse, and the inverse are also represented in Scripture—that is, one might feel love *for* someone or something, feel loved *by* someone or something, and feel *unloving* toward someone or something. Character traits and behaviors related to emotions are also frequently represented. Since the Bible isn't always explicit about emotions, these traits or behaviors are what I consider to be emotion-adjacent words in Scripture, so I included them as well.

The emotion words in Scripture remind us of our connectedness, often appearing as relational and spiritual experiences. I encourage you to resist our modern urge to categorize and completely understand.

Sometimes the emotions listed are intricately bound to the ancient writer's experience of culture and community. It's important to consider their cultural lens as well as our own. I recommend you hold this list with a posture of curiosity, as a way of connecting with our wondrous God.

abhor
afflicted
afraid
aghast
agitated
alarm
aloof
amazed
anguish
anger
annoyed
anxious
appalled
apologetic
astonished
astounded
awake
awe
begrudging
beloved
bereaved
bereft
betrayed
bitter
blameless
boastful
bold
bothered
breathless
broken
brokenhearted
bruised
burdened/laden
calm
captivated
care
cast down/cast off
cheerful
comforted
compassion
compelled
complacent
confident
confounded

confused
considerate
consoled
consumed
contempt
contentious
contrite
courageous
covetous
cramped
crushed
cut to the heart
deceitful
deceived
defiant
delight
derision
desire
desolate
despair
despise
diligent
disappointment
disbelieving
disconnection
discouraged
disgrace
disheartened
dismay
displeased
distracted
distress
divided (in self)
downtrodden
dread
dull
eager
ease
empty
encouraged
enmity
envy
excluded
exhausted

exultant
failing
faint
fear
fear of God
feeble
fierce
firm
flattered
foolish
forgotten
forlorn
forsaken
free
fruitful
fury/furious
generous
glad
gloom
gracious
greedy
grief/grieved
grumbly
guilt/guilty
happy
harassed
hardened
hard/hardhearted
hard pressed
harsh
hate/hated
haughty
heard
heartbroken
heavy
held
helpful
honor
hopeful
hopeless
horror
hostile
humble
humiliated

hurt
ignorant
immovable
impatient
impudent
incensed
indignation
injustice (sense of)
insulted
inviting
jealous
joy
jubilant
languish
loathe
lofty
lonely
longing
love/loved
low
lust
malice
marvel
merciful
merry
mirth
mischievous
misery/miserable
mournful
moved
needy (in need)
offended
oppressed
overcome
overwhelmed
pain
panic
passion
patient
peace
perplexed
pity
pleasant
pleased

pride/proud
prosperous
provoked
quarrelsome
questioning
quiet
rage
rash
rebellious
refreshed
refuge (sense of)
regret
rejected
relief
renewed
repentant
rested
restless
restored
reviled
revived
ruined
ruthless
sad
safe
satisfied
scorn
secretive
secure
seen
shaken
shame (ashamed)
sick with _____
small
solemn
sorrow
sorry
spurned
steady/steadfast
still
stirred up
strengthened/strong
stricken
suffering

supported
surrounded
sympathy
tearful
tender
terror
tested
thankful/thanksgiving
thirsty
thoughtful
threatened
thrilled
tired
trampled
trapped
triumphant
troubled
trust
turmoil
uncertain
unrelenting
unwavering
unworthy
upset
urgent
vehement
vengeance/vengeful
vexation
victorious
vindicated
want
weak
weary
weepy
weighed down
welcoming
wholehearted
willful
willing
withered
woe
wonder
wounded
wrath

wronged
yearning
zeal

DISCUSSION QUESTIONS

Introduction

1. What conversations and complications do you notice as the world responds to the topic of emotion?

2. What conversations and complications do you notice as the Church responds to the topic of emotion?

3. What questions do you have about God and emotion? What questions do you have about emotion in general?

PART 1: BELIEFS ABOUT EMOTIONS

Foundations of Emotion

1. In what ways is it helpful for us to consider emotions apart from our own experience of them?

2. What purpose do you see in our emotions as gifts from God?

3. What would life be like without emotions? (Consider both positive and negative ways.)

The Image of God

1. Read Genesis 1–3. What emotions do you notice in the account of creation and the first sin of humanity? What emotional details do you notice are left out?

2. In what ways is the complexity of God and His emotions challenging for you?

3. Dream for a moment: What do you think emotional wholeness will look like when Jesus restores all things?

Brokenness and Grace

1. Which emotions are most uncomfortable for you? How might those emotions be beneficial in a broken world?

2. Have you ever related to Jonah, challenged by God's mercy and compassion toward certain people or circumstances?

3. How might we benefit from a process-oriented approach to our emotions?

PART 2: MISCONCEPTIONS ABOUT EMOTIONS

Partial Truths

1. What ideas, beliefs, or misconceptions in our culture can you identify that impact the way we view our emotions? Can you follow the trail to learn where any of these ideas, beliefs, or misconceptions originated?

2. Which partial truth about emotions impacts your life or the lives of those you love?

Positive and Negative Emotions

1. How have you experienced this partial truth in your own life or seen it impact someone in your life?

2. What might change about the way we think, feel, or act about emotions if we were honest about this partial truth?

Too Emotional

1. How have you experienced this partial truth in your own life or seen it impact someone in your life?

2. What might change about the way we think, feel, or act about emotions if we were honest about this partial truth?

Unified Facial Response

1. How have you experienced this partial truth in your own life or seen it impact someone in your life?

2. What might change about the way we think, feel, or act about emotions if we were honest about this partial truth?

Regulation

1. How have you experienced this partial truth in your own life or seen it impact someone in your life?

2. What might change about the way we think, feel, or act about emotions if we were honest about this partial truth?

PART 3: WAYS TO PROCESS EMOTIONS

About Emotional Processes

1. What tools do you naturally lean toward to process your emotions?

2. What are some of your personal biases or ways you view the world? How might these impact the way you read emotions in Scripture?

3. This chapter listed defense mechanisms and gave the example of King David using repression in 2 Samuel 11. Which Bible stories come to mind when you consider the other defense mechanisms in this chapter?

Contemplation

1. Take a moment and list what you see in the room around you that you didn't notice when you walked in or sat down.

2. What might people—including you—find uncomfortable about being still and being known by God?

3. Name one emotion that presented itself in your life in the last week. What grace does God have available for that emotion?

Articulation

1. Using a visual or image, how would you describe the five common emotions of happy, sad, angry, scared, and surprised?

2. Why might the unchanging truth of God in affection, comfort, and joy, listed in Philippians 2:1–3, as well as our earthly experience of affection, comfort, and joy both matter to God?

3. Review the list of scriptural articulations of emotion in this chapter. Which stand out to you as surprising or particularly useful for processing emotions?

Exploration

1. What questions about God and faith did you have when you were twelve? Did you have a spiritual mentor or guide to help you answer them?

2. What Bible stories or passages come to mind when you think about processing emotions in a physical way?

3. What are some ways you naturally experience emotions physically? For example, do you cry or feel the need to do something with your fists when you're angry?

Connection

1. What keeps us from sitting with someone in their emotions?

2. While it is a mystery to some extent, what might be some reasons God made humans to be in tune with one another's emotions?

3. Where and when do you see the need for God's grace in the form of boundaries in emotional processing through connection?

PART 4: SPECIFIC EMOTIONS

Forgotten Emotions of Scripture

1. Open to the Psalms or any other book of the Bible, read a chapter or two, and note the emotion words you find. How do you hear these words used in daily life? Have they been forgotten or fallen out of use?

Specific Emotion Chapters

1. Of the emotions discussed in this section—delight, distress, weariness, indignance, contempt, perplexity, and felt compassion—which might be most helpful for you to use in your everyday life to connect the dots between God and your emotions? Why this one in particular?

2. Review the "Notice and Name" section at the end of each chapter to dive deeper into a specific emotion.

Conclusion

1. Which emotions in your life could benefit from applying more of God's gentleness?

2. What shoulds and musts about emotion are you left with after reading? How might God's grace in Jesus Christ answer each of those shoulds and musts?

ACKNOWLEDGMENTS

This was, not surprisingly, an emotional book for me to write. My gratitude is deep and wide, and this list non-exhaustive:

To my mom, my dad, and my sisters for being the first people to make space for my emotions, teaching me love and teaching me boundaries; for Sisters Club meetings and mushroom hunting in the woods; for reminding me that life's hard things and the emotions that come with them won't last forever, and that laughter can coexist with sadness and pain.

To Dave, Macee, Jonah, Jyeva, and Ezekiel for understanding when it's writing season, for warming up the hot tea water again and again, and for embracing our new season where you occasionally bring me snacks rather than the other way around. You all are incredible humans, and I love that I get to know you and discover who God made you to be with the name "Mom" attached.

To Courtney and my Sarahs for spending a disruptive amount of time listening to my ideas and helping me wrestle with an outline, sort through theology, and find the stories that were worth being told but also held purpose and presence to help the reader with all the baggage that comes with the topic of emotions.

To Megan and Genevieve for reminding me that the critics and my inner critic aren't the voices the reader needs to hear, but to allow the Spirit and God's Word to shine bright as I type each page.

To Dr. Nathan Jastram for his thoughts and clarity (where there can be clarity) on the image of God.

To a small group of powerhouse women in Nebraska who have cheered me on in every endeavor, reminding me that my words hold insight and comfort, and that I'm entirely capable when it's hard for me to see my capability.

To my therapy clients who are willing to dig in the trenches of emotion, be creative, and stay connected. Therapy is work, and I'm honored to be a tiny part of the work with you.

To my new office mates and my new faith family in Michigan for making space for me and making space for me to write and practice therapy and be a part of the community and work we have been given together.

To mentors who pour time into you and make you think, especially for Jim and Pat, thanks for being willing to teach me something in every conversation.

To Jamie, Laura, Elizabeth, Holli, Anna, Alex, and the rest of the team, and really the whole CPH family. It is incredible to work with creative professionals who value people being connected with God and one another through communicating God's Word and work in our everyday lives. You are my publishing house heroes.

To the reader for being willing to wrestle, learn, grow, tackle, talk about, poke at, and otherwise reflect on the topic of emotions. I pray this book leaves you hearing the Gospel through and with each emotion a little more often, and bringing the Gospel to the emotions of your people a little more each day.

Also by Heidi Goehmann

Altogether Beautiful: A Study of the Song of Songs
    In this incredible book of the Bible, discover deep spiritual truths, grapple with some of the most uncomfortable topics and questions found in the Bible, and—perhaps best of all—see the fantastic and lavish love our Savior offers us. Videos also available.

The Mighty & The Mysterious: A Study of Colossians
    Walk with Heidi Goehmann through God's Word to the Colossians. Though many things will remain a mystery until we see our Savior face-to-face, readers will discover that God fills them right now in every way, through the mighty and mysterious Body of Christ, the Church. Videos also available.

Finding Hope: From Brokenness to Restoration
    It's time to call brokenness by name. Find tools to identify your story and see God's hope amidst the mess of life. Join Heidi Goehmann on this journey to unveil brokenness together for God's healing.

For more information, visit cph.org.